LESLIE J. TIZARD

GUIDE TO MARRIAGE

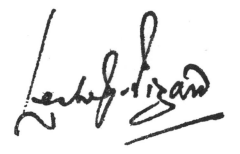

LONDON · UNWIN BOOKS

First Published in January 1948
Reprinted
1948, 1949, 1951, 1953, 1955, 1956
First Published in this Edition 1960
Second Impression 1961
Third Impression 1962
Fourth Impression 1964
Fifth Impression 1965
Sixth Impression 1966
Seventh Impression 1967
Eighth Impression 1968
Ninth Impression 1969
Tenth impression 1970
Eleventh Impression 1971

Paper Edition ISBN 0 04 173004 6
Cloth Edition ISBN 0 04 173003 8

UNWIN BOOKS
*George Allen & Unwin Ltd
Ruskin House, Museum Street
London*

PRINTED IN GREAT BRITAIN
in 10pt Plantin type
BY LOWE AND BRYDONE (PRINTERS) LTD
LONDON

THIS IS WHERE YOU BEGIN!

I hope you won't feel you've been inveigled by false pretences into reading this page. I could, of course, have written *Preface* in the ordinary way, but I'm told that nobody bothers to read prefaces, and if you are proposing to go through this book there really are one or two things I want to say to you before you start.

First of all, you may quite reasonably ask who I am to write a book about marriage and what my qualifications are. Well, at any rate, I'm married myself and have been for eighteen years—which ought to be long enough to learn the way about. And all through those eighteen years I have had a lot to do with young couples looking forward to marriage, with husbands and wives whose marriages have in some way gone awry, and with a great many who have been wonderfully happy—yes, believe it or not, there are still a lot of really successful marriages in spite of the divorce court figures and all you read in the papers. It has been part of my job, I suppose, to listen to their stories and to try to help them with their problems, and I have counted it a privilege to be given their confidence. And then I happen to be chairman of the Marriage Guidance Council in one of our biggest cities, and the Council and its consultants are always dealing with marriage problems of one sort and another—hundreds of them in a year. Those, I am afraid, are about all the qualifications I can lay claim to.

You may ask, too, *why* I have thought it necessary to write a book on marriage. That also is a very sensible question, for in these days there are a lot of books on the subject and a few good ones among them. Well, I've written it because I have not come across just the book I thought was needed—in particular, one which I could recommend to a couple getting ready for marriage and say, 'This book deals with *every* side of marriage.' Don't imagine from this that I think I've written the last word on marriage! When I've done my best it's bound to be pretty inadequate on some aspects of the subject. When you turn over and read 'What It's All About', you'll see that it sets out to cover a tremendous lot of ground—but then marriage does, doesn't it? And you may very well ask how anybody can claim to be an expert on medicine and psychology and finance and architecture and all the rest of it. But I want to give you this assurance. When I've thought it was necessary, I've quite shamelessly picked the brains of experts. For instance, I've pumped Mr C. L. Fielden, F.C.A., about finances, and Mr S. T. Walker, F.R.I.B.A., about furniture and architecture. The appendages to their names guarantee that they *do* know something about those things. In fact, every page in the book has been vetted by an appropriate expert to see that I didn't make any glaring howlers! I am indebted to two doctors, Dr Mary Winfield and Dr C. W. Taylor (Director of Pathology, The Women's Hospital, Birmingham), with whom I have discussed what is especially within their province. But my greatest debt is to my wife. I've written it all, but we have been over every line together and discussed every problem, and, if you find anything useful in the book, it will **very** likely be something of hers which I have put into my own words. Anyway, nobody will be able to say—as sometimes is said of books written by men—that it takes no account of the woman's point of view. She has seen to that! To a great extent, of course, the book is the product of our eighteen years of married life together— of our successes and, not less, of our failures, for we can learn from our failures what *not* to do, and that is always something.

There is one more point. I am quite sure it is useless to write a book like this unless it really gets down to things, calls a spade a spade, and goes into even the most intimate details when necessary. The sort of stuff that used to be written was not only useless; it was a positive menace because it made people think they knew what they needed to know, when they didn't. Some folk may be a bit shocked by the frankness of some of these pages. I want to say that I am dealing all the time with what I *know* to be the real problems of married people because they have discussed them with me. If any-body feels awkward or embarrassed in reading anything in the book, it is because he or she has not attained an adult attitude to sex and has not learned to look upon it objectively as a fact of nature which can be accepted and talked about like anything else which is a fact of nature.

The book is in the form of letters to Jack and Jill. They are an imaginary couple—yet I have met them scores of times, have listened to their hopes and fears, and tried to answer their questions. I send the book on its way with the wish that it may be of use to many Jacks and Jills whom I shall never have the privilege of knowing.

WHAT IT'S ALL ABOUT

So you're going to get engaged!

My dear Jack,

When I opened your letter my eye fell at once on the word 'engaged'. I said to myself, 'The young rascal has kept this very quiet!' and I began to fumble in my pocket to see how funds stood, thinking that you would tell me the date of the wedding before the end of the letter. I find that many men meet a girl and get engaged and married at such a speed that they leave one standing, and, almost before one realizes they *are* married, a lot of them are talking about getting divorced, which—all things considered—isn't very surprising. Did you, by the way, happen to see that remark of Mr Claud Mullins' recently: 'We are soon to have temporary houses. Let us hope that they are not to be occupied by temporary husbands and wives?'

Well, you don't seem to be rushing into anything like that. Honestly, I'm a bit flattered by your letter. A lot of young people have got engaged and *then* asked me to give them advice, but to be asked by anyone to advise him as to whether he should propose to a girl is something nearly new in my experience. If I may say so, without sounding patronizing, I think you are showing sound sense when you decide to discuss things with somebody before you take a step which, if it isn't irrevocable, couldn't be retraced without heart-burnings or even heart-breakings. Of course, in the end you will have to make the decision yourself. If you are half the man I think you are, you are not likely to let anybody else make it for you. But you are right in thinking that somebody with a bit of experience, who has seen the inside of a good many marriages in a way that only doctors, parsons and a few other people do, may be able to help you to sort out your ideas and to avoid a few snags. I will certainly do what I can. Naturally I shall have to talk in rather general terms because I don't really know Jill. I have only met her once—on the day you introduced me to her at the cricket match. I remember I had a feeling that I should hear more about her! And—let me whisper it softly—I'm not altogether surprised that you describe her in your letter as 'a bit of a stunner'. But I'm very glad, for the sake of you both, that she hasn't stunned you so completely that you can't think straight.

When you get time, sit down and tell me all about her. I imagine you won't find it an uncongenial task. Then I'll give you my ideas for what they are worth. I shall not expect you to swallow them all forthwith, but they will give you something to bite on.

Sex attraction and blinkers

WELL, that *was* a letter! After reading it a time or two I felt I had begun to know Jill. You wouldn't expect me to believe that you have given me an impartial portrait, but you are not wearing blinkers as so many people in your situation do.

As I had supposed, it was for both of you love at first sight. That means that it was a case of 'falling' in love and not of moving gently into it by degrees. In such a case it is advisable at some point to try to arrest the 'fall'—to pull the rip-cord so that you can float gently down and have a chance to see what sort of country you are likely to land in.

Love at first sight generally means that a tremendously strong sexual attraction begins to work instantaneously. Sex attraction is a bit of a mystery. A man meets hundreds of girls, some of whom are certainly 'attractive', and is not seriously disturbed by any of them. Then he bumps into one who, in a twinkling, knocks him off his balance, upsets his appetite, turns him into a dreamer and does all sorts of other things to him. Some seem to be attracted by a pretty face, some by a well-proportioned figure, others by beauty in some particular feature, by a certain quality of voice, and so on. However it works, a strong sex attraction pretty effectively suspends for the time being our powers of rational judgment so far as the object of it is concerned.

I think there is something distinctively 'chancy' about sex attraction. A couple who meet and fall in love at first sight on Wednesday might have met and parted unscathed on Saturday. That is largely a matter of glands. A wise doctor has told us how Antony and Cathrine fell in love and *why* it happened at their first meeting just as it did:

And so that night, superficially because the conversation of

Antony had appeared unusual, primarily because that more generous and romantic phase of Cathrine's physical cycle prevailed, Antony, when he left her at the door, experienced a reciprocated sympathetic pressure of his hand. In this way began the romance of Cathrine and Antony. Each felt attracted to the other, and each remained oblivious to the *cause* which had produced those particular features which attracted. The last thing which Cathrine would suspect was a nervous over-sensitivity in Antony. The first thing which Antony would naturally appraise was Cathrine's consideration and sympathy. The phases of her moon camouflaged the supreme defect of Cathrine, prolonged habit concealed the most powerful weakness of Antony. And in this utterly deceptive moment—the deceptive nature of which neither the man nor the girl had ever been *taught* by their parents to understand—a spark was lit which was destined to burn away the very life and happiness of both.

Of course, with more fortunate Antonies and Cathrines that spark might kindle a glow which would warm them both their whole lives through. But there is simply no telling in the moment when the spark is first struck; it feels the same either way.

It often happens that a man and a girl do not realize at first that it is sex which is exerting such a pull on them. A man may even regard a girl for a time as a sort of ethereal goddess whom he would not dream of approaching in any obviously sexual way. But sex is at work, and the tragedy of Antony and Cathrine (as well as of thousands in real life) is a warning of the danger of building anything blindly on sex alone.

Let me be clear that I am not belittling sexual attraction or suggesting for a moment that it is evil. It is good and it is necessary. Indeed, you can't have a complete marriage without it. I came to the conclusion long ago that, speaking generally, there is not too much sex love in marriage, but too little. You can set down the physical attraction which Jill and you feel for each other as one of your biggest assets. What people are *capable* of feeling in that way varies, of course, but I don't think a couple ought to marry unless mutual physical desire is there. Sometimes it may come to consciousness slowly. They may be drawn together in the first place by a common interest in books, music, rambling, dogs, politics or what you will, and only gradually do they become aware that something more than friendship is bringing them closer. It may be a long time in dawning, especially if a lad and a girl have known each other for years and have been more or less brought up together. And it is probably true that some women are not *fully* aroused sexually until they are actually married. But it is certainly foolish for a couple to marry unless they do feel a mutual attraction, and to bank on the hope that desire may arise after marriage, when it has been absent all through courtship, is simply asking for trouble. A marriage which has no foundation of sexual love is likely to be as shaky as one which has no other foundation, and if later on one of the partners meets a person who is capable of arousing the dormant sex feeling, the marriage will almost certainly crash in ruins. At any rate, nothing more than a façade will remain intact to hide the unspeakable misery behind it.

The point I am trying to make in this letter is that you can count the physical attraction you both feel as one of your blessings—and not the least of them; but the strength of it makes it doubly imperative that you should be sure other things are not lacking, which are just as necessary to a happy marriage. Sex love alone might give you a rapturous honeymoon, but it wouldn't give you much more. I doubt whether it would give you even that, and you would probably go to the home (where you have to spend not a fortnight, remember, but a whole lifetime) with a nasty sense of disillusionment, and feeling as irritable with each other as a couple of bears with sore heads.

The only sound basis for marriage, you see, is a love which includes sex—but an enormous lot besides!

What love is not

———————————————•———————————————

YOU were quite right to take me up about the end of my last letter and to point out that I had better define my terms. For, as you say, the word 'love' can mean anything—or nothing. It can, in fact, stand for the sort of tosh served up in the worst kind of Hollywood film, which is a profanation of the word. In common parlance it may be used of mere lust or sentimentality, and at the other extreme it may denote the sublimest thing of which a human being is capable: the devotion of the whole self—body, mind, heart and will—to another person.

Well, I don't pretend I can give you a pat *definition* of real love, but I can tell you some things that it is—and a good many that it isn't.

Let me be quite personal. To love Jill means to care for her because of what she is and not because of anything she can give you or do for you. One man may make an alliance with a girl (that is what it amounts to) because he thinks she will be an asset to him in his profession, wherein he has great ambitions. Another, who would like to cut a figure, looks for a woman who will be a charming hostess. Another, who feels inferior, wants to marry a handsome wife so that he can boost himself up when he introduces her to his friends. The look in his eyes will say, 'You can't show me anything as good as that—and she's all *mine* ! So you had better revise your opinion of me.' None of these really knows what love is.

A cynical Frenchman, writing about friendship, said: 'What is commonly called friendship is no more than a partnership, a reciprocal regard for another's interest, an exchange of good offices, in a word a traffic wherein self-love always proposes to be the gainer.' The 'love' which sometimes brings about a marriage is that kind of thing. But in such cases the regard for self-interest may not even be reciprocal; one party may quite blatantly exploit the other and give nothing in return.

Very well then, the love which Jill and you have for each other is not a traffic of self-interest. You love her for *herself*. And by 'herself' I do not mean any brilliant gifts she may happen to have, or physical beauty, or a rippling laugh, or whatever it was which knocked you sideways when you first set eyes on her. For one reason or another she might lose all those. Time will inevitably take toll of her youthful loveliness, though, mind you, middle age and even old age can have a beauty of their own, and I suspect Darby and Joan, if they have been real lovers, see beauty in each other until the end of the chapter. You see, you did not really love Jill when you first saw her and she caused palpitations. How could you? You only knew that here was a beautiful thing which some-how appealed to the male in you, though you may also have sensed by intuition some of her qualities. Only gradually could you come to know her and care for her as a *person*. If you have learned to love her in that way, you have the kind of love which will deepen as the years go on, even if something—illness or accident, perhaps —should take away her more superficial charms.

Now, all that may sound rather romantic, so let me add quickly that to romanticize love is a snare and a delusion. I daresay we are not so much given to it as the Victorians were, but it remains a danger when people are very much in love. It is a good thing for young love to have its head a little in the clouds, but it needs to have its feet planted very firmly on the earth. I was speaking about these things once, and a fellow in the audience asked me how a man could tell whether he really loved a girl or was merely swept off his feet by physical attraction. My reply was something like this: 'She won't always look as she did at the picnic on the river or at the dance last night. You had better try to imagine what she is like in the morning with her make-up off and her hair all over the place. You had better picture what she might look like in the middle of a bilious attack, when her face is green, or when she is hot and worried and the baby is being sick all over her! If you feel certain you would love her just as much then, that you would want to be with her even more then than you do now, when she is fresh and full of the joy of life—go ahead. As the immortal song has it, "That's not the moon, that's love, my son!" ' An old man sitting in the front row, an intimate friend of mine, whose marriage has always been wonderfully happy, nodded his head vigorously and said, 'Hear, hear!' (By the way, I think any man whose girl persistently makes-up ought to have the right to see her at least once minus lipstick and all the rest of it before he proposes. It might save disappointment later on.)

But the peril is not confined to idealising physical beauty. It is just as dangerous to endow the beloved with all conceivable gifts and graces. If limitations and weaknesses do not become apparent before marriage, they pretty certainly will afterwards. If a couple have set each other on pedestals, they may feel badly let down and will soon be saying bitterly, 'You are not the man (or woman) I thought you were,' with the corollary (spoken or implied), 'I would never have married you if I had known.' They ought to have realized long before that they were both bits of ordinary humanity with plenty of faults and some good qualities mixed up with them. They should have accepted each other on that basis. That does not mean, of course, that they should accept their own or each other's failings as inevitable or incurable. If they have not expected or demanded perfection, they can help each other to overcome weaknesses with tolerance and good humour.

Here is another point about loving a person for himself or herself alone. It's an odd thing that some people choose a husband or wife because they are looking for somebody else! A man may marry a particular woman because he is seeking for one to take the place of his mother or (less frequently) his sister to whom he was deeply attached. The poor wife will be in for a bad time if she is expected to take the place of a doting mother fussing over a spoiled child. Again, a woman may marry a particular man, especially a much older one, because she wants a father rather than a husband. It is not surprising that in cases like these a husband may turn out to be sexually impotent or a wife frigid, i.e., unable to make any sexual response. Some wives want to find in their husbands 'children' whom they can mother. That suits some husbands very well (more's the pity), but others find it galling. Of course, nearly every wife wants to mother her husband sometimes, and, if he understands, he won't object; it's all a matter of degree. These cases can be very difficult. Generally the man or woman, who is looking for a mother or father 'substitute', will be quite unconscious of it. But if a man has any reason to suspect that a woman wants him to take the place of her father, or a woman that a man is seeking his mother in her, they will be well advised not to marry, however much they care for each other, until things have been sorted out— and that may be a job for an expert psychologist.

There is one other kind of substitution. When a lover has been lost, either through death or the breaking off of a love affair, a man or woman may quickly find a new lover, but the new one is really a substitute for the old. It is not unknown in those circumstances for a husband or wife in their marital relations to imagine that inter- course is taking place not with the present but the former lover. If that happens, there will be trouble ahead—nervous and otherwise. A more common danger, when an engagement has been broken off, is that in hurt pride a man or girl will rush into the arms of the first person who is available. It is a way of saying to a faithless lover, 'I'll show you', and also a means of reassurance that the power to attract has not yet been lost. I have known a man and a girl, both of whom had been jilted, rush into each other's arms without really caring for each other at all. What could be the end of it ? It is terribly dangerous to marry on the rebound from a romance which has gone awry. People who have been involved in a broken engage- ment ought not to become betrothed again until they have got over the hurt and disappointment and can think straight—and that sometimes takes quite a time.

I seem to have been saying a good deal about what love is not. It is time I said a little about what it is, but I will leave that for my next letter.

What love really is

I SAID in my last letter that to love Jill means to care for her as a *person*. If you really love her you will always respect her as a personality. That is a principle which is quite fundamental to all our human relationships, but nowhere is it so vital as in the intimacies of marriage and home life. To respect a man as a personality means always to treat him as a human being, who has certain inalienable rights because of the very fact that he *is* a human being. It means treating him always as a person and never as a thing, or, as the philosophers put it, as an end in himself and never as a means to your own ends. There isn't any need to enlarge on that because everybody knows in his own experience the difference between being treated as a person and as a thing. Somebody has said it is just the difference between being *told* to do something and being *asked* to do it. I am afraid many husbands and wives do not always respect one another as persons, and I don't know that one sex is any more addicted to the fault than the other. In the realm of sex men are, in the very nature of the case, the chief offenders. It is not treating a woman as a *person* when a man *uses* her for his own sexual gratification—but I shall have more to say about that one of these days. Well, then, a fundamental part of love is this respect for personality; without it, no matter what you feel, love isn't possible.

The love of husband and wife ought to include respect of another kind. We ought to respect even a despicable rogue as a personality —i.e. we ought to remember that he still has a right to be treated as a person and not as a thing. But if two people are thinking of getting married they ought to be able to respect each other's characters. If they can't, no matter how strong the sexual pull, or how entertaining they find each other, they should never consider joining their lives together. I am not suggesting that they should think each other perfect; remember what I said about idealizing. You can respect a person who has faults which stick out a mile—at any rate, *some* faults. It is asking for trouble when a woman takes a husband, whom she doesn't respect, because she thinks she will 'make a man of him'. It doesn't often work, anyhow. She will probably find she has over-estimated her power of influencing him, and he will resent 'being done good to'. Most likely he will go to the devil in his own way and she will go through life feeling a martyr. (Of course, some people like to feel martyrs!) It is a good thing to befriend people whose characters we cannot really respect, to be kind and helpful to them, but we ought to draw the line at marrying them.

I think a useful test is to ask, 'How should I like this man or woman to be the parent of my children?' You would not like to have a woman for the mother of your children whom you couldn't honestly respect—one, for example, who might be an amusing toy (until you got tired of her!), but who was as shallow as a woman could be. And you wouldn't like to saddle your children with a mother, who was none of their choosing, whom they might not be able to respect either. (By the way, we can't *demand* respect from our children; we can only *deserve* it. It is just nonsense to say, 'You ought and you shall respect me *because* I am your father.' The mere fact that a man performs a sexual act, perhaps without thinking of a child, and even determined not to have one if he can help it, doesn't establish any obligation on the child to think him a noble fellow if he isn't.)

Another characteristic of true love is a desire to give and to receive. Yes, both. I don't mean that love demands so much for so much. Love will give all it has to give even when no return is possible. But it is a false notion that love—married love at any rate—is all giving. A lover receives gladly even as he gives gladly. Of course, there are people who want to give all the time and who just don't know how to receive graciously. Some want to do all the giving because it satisfies their desire for power. They are trying to make people feel dependent on them so that they themselves can feel superior. And they won't receive anything in return because that would make them feel dependent themselves, and therefore inferior. Some parents will slave for their children, not because

they really love them unselfishly, but because they want to bind
the children to them, and, if the children do not seem properly
impressed and grateful, they will say, 'See how much I have done
for you'—which is sheer spiritual blackmail. Husbands and wives
sometimes try the same tactics on each other. In real love there is
no thought of trying to place the receiver of a gift or service in your
debt. You give happily and gladly simply because you love. But,
since it makes you happy to give to a person you love, you won't
deny the person who loves you the same happiness. And you will
make him feel that what he has to give is worth having and
means something to you. That is how love ought to give and
receive in marriage.

And love means friendship. Remember the love of husband and
wife has to last a lifetime, and it won't unless they are friends. They
must have a lot of interests in common. A wise American has said,
'The emotion of love is not self-sustaining; it endures only when
the lovers love many things together and not merely one another.
It is the understanding that love cannot be isolated from the business
of living which is the enduring wisdom of the institution of marriage.' That does not mean, of course, that one must not have *any*
interests and tastes which the other does not share. Jack Spratt and
his wife did not have exactly the same likings in the matter of meat,
but history does not record that they were an unhappy couple.
Indeed, their complementary tastes seem to have worked out very
satisfactorily. Given proper understanding and tolerance, there is
room for wide difference of views even on important subjects.
After all, husband and wife remain individuals and ought not to be
mere replicas of each other. But the area of common interests
needs to be wide and to include the deep things of life. A common
liking for dancing or films is a pretty meagre foundation for a
friendship that has to last a lifetime. I think a husband and wife, in
order to achieve such a friendship, need to be more or less equally
matched in intelligence. I do not mean that they should necessarily
have had the same education and certainly not that they should be
experts in the same subjects. Intelligence is not the same thing as
'education'. If a really intelligent man or woman is yoked to a dull
partner, both of them will probably suffer from boredom when
superficial attractions begin to wear thin. Friendship means the

sharing of life, and to be complete it must mean the sharing of intellectual and spiritual life as well as comradeship in the thousand-and-one affairs of every day.

So, to sum up: love equals friendship plus sex. Both are indispensable, but of the two I think friendship is the more important because the lasting quality of love depends upon it. They are a happy couple who can say:

'We shall be lovers when the last door shuts,
But, what is better still, we shall be friends.'

Engagement

CONGRATULATIONS to you both! I am sure you have done the right thing, and I was particularly glad to read, 'Neither Jill nor I have the slightest misgiving.' That is how it should be. It is a great pity when somebody gets engaged with one-half of the mind raising doubts and asking, 'Will it turn out all right or am I going to regret it?' That is a poor way to enter on a life which demands, for its complete success, the absolute committal of one's whole self. Among the congratulations you will receive there will probably be a few commiserations. Most people who offer you their 'sympathy' won't, of course, mean to be taken seriously; those jokes, like the others about mothers-in-law, are part of the stock-in-trade of popular humour. But you or—much more likely—Jill may run into the middle-aged cynic who thinks it is her (or his) business to 'disillusion' the young about marriage. Some woman, whose marriage has been a mess through her misfortune or fault, may take it upon herself to 'enlighten' Jill. She will very likely tell her, in particular, that the whole sexual side of marriage will be nothing but misery, and will perhaps warn her that all men are selfish beasts. Sometimes it is even a bride's mother who imparts this 'enlightenment', leaving it—presumably to achieve the maximum effect—until the very morning of the wedding day. People whose marriages have gone awry, especially those who have had no sexual satisfaction, often have their outlook completely warped. They think there are no happy marriages, whereas there are thousands of them—only they are not news. These soured cynics, who are often more to be pitied than blamed, ought to take a vow of silence rather than allow themselves to plant misgivings in the minds of young people, who should enter into marriage with unalloyed hope and confidence.

However, I think it would take a cart-load of cynics to upset Jill and you. You have taken the plunge without any shudderings on the brink, and I expect you had all the more confidence because you took the trouble to have a good straight think about things.

You ask me how long I think an engagement ought to be. There is no short answer to that question; the desirable length varies with circumstances and individuals. I take it that the object of a period of engagement is twofold: (1) to give a couple an opportunity to get to know each other better and to reach an understanding on all important matters, and (2) to afford time for the practical arrangements which have to be made for setting up a home. So far as the first is concerned, the length of the engagement should depend on how well the couple know each other already. You notice I say not how *long* they have known each other, but how *well*. Sometimes a married pair have told me that they can't go on together any longer because they find that they have nothing in common. An obvious question is, 'How long were you engaged?' Sometimes it turns out to have been a rushed job, but surprisingly often the engagement was of considerable length. So I say, 'Well, surely that gave you enough time to find out whether you were suited and had much in common. How did you spend the time?' and often I get the answer, 'Oh, we used to go to the pictures and dances sometimes, but you don't get to know much about each other like that.' Of course not. During the engagement a couple ought to get down to things—to everything, in fact. They should get to know just what they think about home life, religion, sex, children, birth control, money, careers and so on. All these things, and a host of others, ought to be talked out with complete frankness and with the help of experienced advice when necessary. No doubt some folk (though not many young folk nowadays, I fancy) would be shocked at the notion of an unmarried lad and girl talking about sex and birth-control, but, if they knew how much suffering arises after marriage because these things have *not* been talked about, they might revise their ideas.

An engagement ought to be a chance not only to discuss ideas, but to get to know each other's characters. That means having the courage to be honest. Courtship, you see, is a time of showing-off. Stifle your protests! All living things above the jelly-fish level do it! Birds strut about and display their plumage or show off their voices. (Jill will point out that it is generally the male who does this.) In primitive society, dancing as a means of self-display takes a great place in courtship. In New Guinea no words are spoken; a suitor dances before the girl, making athletic bounds and going through the movements of spearing and so on. (What a paradise for the strong, silent man!) In other countries it is the girl who dances in such a way as to show off her sexual attractions, and then she taps on the shoulder of the man of her choice. I have read that even the modern waltz was originally the closing act of a dramatic dance representing 'the romance of love, the seeking and the fleeing'. In courtship most of us try to make an impression by every art and artifice at our command. We display all the strength, cleverness and beauty we have, and sometimes contrive to produce the illusion of a little more. That's nature, and it is all quite according to the rules of the ancient game of love. But during an engagement a couple should reach a tacit understanding that all posing and striving after effect will be abandoned. That degree of frankness is not, however, always reached even after marriage. Some husbands and wives go on through life keeping up a pose and enduring a sense of strain because of the fear of giving themselves away. It is a bad business when they have not enough confidence in each other just to be themselves.

I think, too, that there ought to be complete frankness about the past, if there has been a 'past'. If often happens, in these days, that one or both have had previous sexual experience. If both of them have, neither can reasonably be shocked. (Some men still seem to think that sexual laxity is to be condoned in a man and condemned in a girl; it is partly a hangover from the time when a woman was thought to be the property of a man.) But there is the possibility that the two may have had different standards or that one of them may have had a lapse in a foolish moment. The writer of one of the best books on marriage seems to me unsound on this point. He says that the unusually frank and honest person may tell too much. 'It may cause mental conflict and lead one partner to lose some respect for the other.' There is certainly a risk in being honest in such a situation, but it may be that the risk of not telling the whole truth is a good deal greater, quite apart from the question of what is ethically right. One partner will feel that he or she is concealing something and may dread that one day, in some unexpected way, it may be discovered—in which case the damage will certainly be greater. And, anyhow, to retain respect by concealing something which the other partner would feel he or she had a right to know looks rather like keeping it under false pretences. The only sound basis for marriage is complete trust, and the fact that one has shown trust by telling what it was not easy to tell ought to call forth a corresponding trust in the other. If it doesn't, perhaps it is just as well after all that it has been told, for the couple will be forced to ask whether they have between them the mutual confidence which would justify them in going forward to marriage. I don't know whether Jill or you have anything of this sort to tell, but, if you have, my advice to you is to get it off your chests. If there is anything, keep it in perspective, and remember it happened before you knew and loved each other.

I have been talking about the engagement as a time of getting to know each other, but it ought also to be a time of getting to know yourselves, and there you can help each other. I don't mean that an engaged couple should form themselves into a mutual criticism society (which is even worse than a mutual admiration society!), but they can occasionally point things out in a kindly and good-humoured way and at the right times and places. Real love isn't blind; it is only sexual passion which *cannot* see, and a love unsure of itself which *dare* not see. Self-knowledge means seeing yourself through somebody else's eyes, and it is useful to see yourself through the eyes of the person you propose to live with. The engagement, then, ought to be a time of self-adjustment as well as of adjustment to the future partner. It has been said that a man cannot be happily married to another until he is happily married to himself—in other words, until he has resolved his own problems and conflicts and achieved inner harmony. There is a good deal of truth in that.

The other purpose of the engagement period, I suggested, is to allow time for the severely practical business of setting up a home. Again, the interval required will obviously vary. I think, however, that one thing is clear. It is better to wait a little longer, if it means marrying without financial anxiety and with a home to yourselves instead of one shared with others, especially if the others are 'in-laws'. In their understandable longing to settle down together at the first possible moment, young people are apt to think they can be in heaven under any conditions, but sometimes they find they have blighted their early happiness because things prove intolerable. On the other hand, of course, they ought not to wait until they can have everything they want. There is a great deal to be said for marrying young.

To sum it all up: I think the best arrangement is a fairly long preliminary courtship and then an engagement which is no longer than it needs to be. A long-drawn-out engagement often puts an intolerable sexual strain on a young couple who are very much in love. Americans are rather good at investigating these problems by using the questionnaire method and reducing them to statistics. Two of their authorities say that on the whole, and with exceptions, a courtship of three to five years (including the engagement) results in the highest percentage of good adjustment. That seems sound sense. They also say that companionship tested by time appears to be a better basis for successful marriage than the emotional feeling of certainty inspired by short-lived romantic love. Beyond question they are right about that.

VI

Sex experience before marriage?

YOUR last letter contains a pretty tall order. You want me to go into the whole question of sex during the engagement because you think Jill and you are going to find it a difficult problem to handle, and because people seem to have such different ideas on the whole matter that you hardly know where you stand. You are quite right in inferring from what I have said about the sexual strain of a long engagement that I think it is best not to have sexual intercourse before marriage. And I've no doubt you are right when you say that, from all you've heard, most of the fellows you work among would hoot at my ideas; and Jill isn't far from the truth, either, when she says that goes for a great many of the girls in her office.

It is quite certain that an enormous number of young people in these days do have intercourse before marriage, but that doesn't prove it is either right or advisable. By the way, don't take quite all you hear from people about their sexual exploits as gospel. Most of it (stripped of its trimmings) is probably more or less true, but people do boast about things they have never done and, in some cases, are never likely to do. I remember a boy at school who achieved a considerable reputation among us as a Don Juan. We lesser fry held him in some awe because of his reputed conquests and regarded him as no end of a fellow. But, of course, we only had his word for it all. We accepted it willingly enough because of our lack of real knowledge and because we wanted him to go on with his tales, but, looking back, I suspect he was bluffing all the time. Boasting about sexual exploits is a way of making an impression in some circles, and therefore people do it for the same reason that an adolescent, who feels inferior and lacks confidence, swears, talks smut, and smokes a pipe. It is a safe guess that some who do most bragging have never had any sexual affairs at all.

But let's get back to Jill and you. It seems to me that the problem of sexual behaviour during engagement boils down, like so many other things, to the question of where you are going to draw the line.

Ideas about these things have changed a good deal. There was a time when a couple obeying the conventions of 'nice' society hardly saw each other alone before marriage, and a girl was laced into her clothes like a knight in armour! That did not prevent people kicking over the traces sometimes, for where there's a will there's a way. And it certainly did not mean that they were all paragons of sexual purity. It was not thought in any way remarkable, for example, if a highly respectable man and the father of a family had a mistress. (Sometimes he could plead in extenuation that his wife had been brought up to think that no 'nice' woman was capable of sex feelings. Some men have always made the most of the real or alleged frigidity of their wives. 'My wife doesn't understand me' is still a common and often effective line of appeal to unwary girls.)

In these days freedom between the sexes is about as untrammelled as it could be. A lad and a girl can work together, play together, dance half the night without a chaperon, and share all sorts of activities and amusements. On a summer evening or at the week-end he can take her on his tandem or motor-cycle or in his sports car to a place miles from anywhere, where they can sunbathe in a state not far removed from nature, and nobody but Mrs Grundy will turn a hair. Now, there is a great deal to be said for that from several points of view. There is always a place for modesty, but it is a good thing for a couple to feel at ease with each other under those conditions. Many children, even in these days, grow up with inhibitions against nakedness, and many of us who have to sort out marriage tangles not infrequently find it is one of the barriers to achieving spontaneity in wedded life.

There is another aspect of the matter which I must mention. In these days there is a great deal of what the Americans call 'necking' and 'petting'. Those terms cover every degree of physical intimacy, including direct stimulation of the sexual organs—everything, in short, which can be, and ought to be, preliminary to sexual union. No doubt there has always been 'petting', but female fashions nowadays make it easy and sometimes positively invite it. Girls often use the freedom, which modern fashions give them, to exploit their sexual attractions in ways which make self-control unnecessarily difficult for men. That isn't fair.

I have been trying to point out that there is a lot to be said for the freedom of modern manners and fashions, but they do create a great deal of sexual stimulation, to say nothing of all the commercialized eroticism which is thrust at us every day of our lives.

Now, Jill and you will feel, as your engagement goes on, that you want an ever-increasing degree of physical intimacy. That is quite right and natural. I should be profoundly disturbed if you told me it were not so. You will have to make up your minds as to just how much liberty you are going to allow each other. If you reach an understanding about it, either of you can gently pull the other up if necessary. You had better decide where your limits are, because, if you don't, two people as much in love as you are may find that you have been swept away from your moorings, and you will end up by going all the way without really meaning it.

I can hear you saying, with half your mind at any rate, 'Well, why not ? Would there be any great harm in it ?'

Quite frankly, I think it would be less wrong than thousands of acts of intercourse which take place in marriage. There is, and can be, only one adequate reason for union, and that is that two people really love each other. I believe that, when one person *uses* another as an instrument for sexual gratification in the absence of love, it is wrong, and the fact that they wear wedding rings doesn't make any difference. A greater wrong against personality has been committed than when a lad and girl are so much in love that they just get swept away.

But that is not to say that to surrender to your urge would be either wise or right, and I don't think it would.

For one thing, Jill might have a baby. Modern birth-control methods are pretty effective, but nobody pretends that they are a hundred per cent certain, and, if you let yourself get suddenly swept away, you won't have anything at hand anyway. You may say that, if a child were born as the result of your love, it could not be a very great sin to create one even out of wedlock. There are more ways than one of looking at that. But even if Jill and you felt no particular shame or guilt about the situation (and you probably would, no matter how modern and emancipated you think your-selves!) you would most likely get married in a hurry, and that would cloud the happiness of making all the preparations and the enjoyment of the first little while alone in your very own home. And even if you are so very 'modern' that you can cock a snook at con-vention, you would cause a great deal of distress and anxiety to friends and relations who still have some regard for the old standards. After all, that would not be exactly kind, and I think you would blame yourselves for being selfish and not waiting.

But, I grant you, you would probably avoid conception. So what? Well, if you have intercourse, you won't be playing fair with Jill, and, only to a lesser degree, she won't be playing fair with you. You've got to bear in mind something which one day I'll say more about. It is pretty certain that Jill has a considerable capacity for sexual feeling. But she may not be fully aroused sexually, and, if you two have intercourse, you may let loose in her urges and desires which may be a perfect torment to her. You see, sexual feeling *can* be something deeper in a woman than in a man. I am not sug-gesting that it is an easy thing for a man to control, but I am sure it may get a woman churned up from the depths of her nature in a way that most men never experience. Once a woman is fully awakened and has known intercourse her desires may be torture to her unless she can satisfy them again. That means there might be a continual state of tension in you both, and between you, unless you were prepared to satisfy your desire whenever it threatened to become intolerable. A great many people, who have intercourse during the engagement, don't really mean to repeat it. They are swept away, or try it out of curiosity, or in order, as they think, to discover whether they are 'suited to each other'. They don't reckon that they may be letting loose something which they can't control. (Incidentally, if some of the fellows in your office who boast about their powers as Don Juans, and who think they know everything, only knew a little more, they might stop and think. To awaken all the sex capacity of a woman, and then to leave her, is a species of cruelty quite up to concentration camp standard. People like doctors and parsons, who have to deal with these personal problems, are familiar enough with the plight of women who have been stimulated and then abandoned with no immediate hope of marriage, and often with no remote prospect either. They suffer tortures of one sort and another, and it is terribly difficult to help them.)

Again, remember it is just possible, for all that you are so much in love and seem so perfectly suited to each other, that Jill and you may not marry after all. I grant you that the likelihood of a slip betwixt cup and lip seems extremely remote, but you can't say it couldn't happen. If, later on, you both wanted to marry other partners, wouldn't you feel better about it if you had never given yourselves to anybody before? As I said in a previous letter, if Jill or you have had any affair in the past, don't take it too tragically, but I doubt if you could deny that you would both like to feel that your first complete sexual experience was with each other.

I think, too, that if you have intercourse before you are married you may give yourselves a great and unnecessary disappointment. Popular novelists have a good deal to answer for in that they cause young people to get hold of a lot of quite erroneous ideas about sexual intercourse. Copulation generally seems to take place before the story has fairly got under way, and almost invariably it would appear to be all romance and rapture and completely successful—even when neither has had any experience before! Such novelists would claim that they are realists—and that is exactly what they are *not*. If they were realists they would say that these first 'romantic' sex acts in the heat of passion are often clumsy and fumbling affairs in which union is not achieved at all, and, if it is, the girl is quite possibly physically hurt. If they told the realistic truth, these novelists would say that the end of it is often enough not a happy and contented couple breathing 'How wonderful!' but two disappointed and perhaps humiliated and resentful people wishing they hadn't done it. I don't mean that the beginning of the full sex life must inevitably be like that. I am saying that it is the kind of thing which is very likely to happen if the couple let themselves get swept off their feet by passion.

I think I hear you saying, 'Well, if there are likely to be difficulties, isn't it better to get over them during the engagement, so that we can start married life without any snags of that sort?' That sounds plausible, but it might not work out very well. You must remember that the whole psychological situation would be different from what it will be when you are married. In the back of your minds there would very likely be the dread of an 'accident', and a sense of guilt, however much you tried to repress these things. Sexual union would not be free from all misgivings and anxiety as it ought to be, and can be, between married people. And if sexual adjustment were not quickly and easily achieved you might lose confidence and get impatient with each other, even to the point of wondering whether you had better break off the engagement; whereas those same difficulties tackled with patience and understanding (remember those two words), when the bond of marriage had already been forged, would probably not be really serious. It is true that intercourse before marriage might occasionally avoid the tying together for life of two people, who never could achieve adjustment, but I am sure happiness is in most cases likely to be secured by waiting. The American investigators, to whom I referred in a previous letter, found that on the average husbands and wives who had had no sexual experience before marriage had the highest 'happiness scores'; those who had had intercourse only with each other came next and those who were promiscuous brought up the rear. They are speaking not as moralists, but as scientific investigators who, as such, have no concern with the ethics of the business.

It is, of course, important to find out whether you are likely to be sexually well adapted to your partner. It won't make for happiness if a volcano is mated to an iceberg! But these things can be gauged pretty accurately without actual intercourse. If there is the same kind of mutual responsiveness in the limited love-making of courtship, there is no reason to suppose it will not be there in the fuller expression which is to come later. And if a couple are equipped with patience and knowledge (I'll write you some letters about that later on) they will have every chance of achieving sexual harmony quite soon in their married life.

By the way, some people who think they are 'modern', and even an occasional doctor, will advise a man who is nervous about whether he will be able to perform the sex act satisfactorily after he is married to go and 'find a woman' with whom he can try it out beforehand. (Quite a lot of men are afraid they will not be 'potent', and nearly always this fear is groundless.) If a man takes that advice and picks up a woman of easy virtue or goes to a regular prostitute, he may find that he has increased his fears instead of losing them. A feeling of guilt or of disgust at some sordidness may make him actually unable to have intercourse, whereas he would have been perfectly potent with his wife. His increased anxiety, because of his actual failure, may cause him difficulties in marriage which he need never have had. (As I believe you have plenty of the finer feelings, I leave you to say just what you think of any man who would treat another person so blatantly as a mere *thing*. The fact that he pays her for the use of her body doesn't make the least difference.)

I could say quite a lot about our responsibility for preserving the sanctity of marriage as the only sound foundation of social life. Everybody who indulges in sex experience outside marriage, for whatever reason, is doing his bit to undermine the foundations. But this letter is long enough already, and we'll let it go at that.

Well, my advice to Jill and you is to allow yourselves all reasonable freedom in your love-making during your engagement, but to have such an understanding that you can help each other not to go so far that you make things harder than they need be. If you give way to desires which are, of course, quite natural, you will create for yourselves difficulties and anxieties. And, anyhow, marriage will mean more to you if you keep the final expression of your love until then. As to the notion that previous experiments are necessary to happy marriage, it is most pernicious nonsense, as a lot of people could tell you from their own bitter experience. Of course, you need knowledge, and a great deal of it, but sexual adventures won't provide you with it.

VII

Moods

I AM sorry last Saturday's expedition wasn't quite the huge success you anticipated, because I know how much you were both looking forward to it. You seem to think it was all Jill's fault, which may or may not be the truth, the whole truth, and nothing but the truth. Perhaps she has her own point of view—but we'll let that pass! As you see it, Jill seemed to be in a queer mood when you started. That meant, I suppose, that you felt a bit deflated and disappointed and possibly weren't as patient as you might have been. It is terribly difficult to put up with other people's moods, especially when we can't see any reason for them, or when they turn out awkwardly and spoil something which promised to be good. You don't say what sort of a mood Jill's was, so I can't say anything about that, but you've given me an opportunity to say a few things about moods in general, which may be useful.

Of course, we are all moody people. Life would be a dreadful business if we weren't. Imagine living in a country where the sun was everlastingly beating down from a perfectly clear, blue sky. Some of the men who spent a good part of the last war in that sort of place said it 'got them down'. They found themselves longing for a few clouds or even a good old London fog—though, no doubt, they did their share of cursing our queer, changeable climate when they were in it. It seems to me it would be a dull, monotonous business if everybody were always in exactly the same mood. If all of us were always perfectly placid, it would be like living in a field of cabbages! And wouldn't it be dreadful to serve a life sentence with a person who insisted on being everlastingly hearty? Moods add a great deal to the variety and interest of life, though, of course, you can have too much a of good thing, and some moods aren't good at any time.

If we are above the vegetable level, then, we are subject to moods.

Some people are more 'moody' than others. They change from one mood to another more quickly and unaccountably, and the variations are more marked. That is partly a matter of temperament. Now, we can't change temperament. That is handed out to us at birth, and we've got to live with it until the end of the chapter, whether we like it or not. But that does not mean we are helplessly at the mercy of temperament, as people seem to think when they say, 'That's how I'm made, and I can't be any different.' As a psychologist points out, our temperaments are given us, but our characters we make—'the use we make of our temperaments constitutes our character, and that use, after all, is what makes our personalities, not the temperament itself.' So it won't do to say, 'I'm a moody person, and you must put up with it.' We haven't any right to adopt that 'take it or leave it' attitude, when our moods make other people miserable. But we ought to recognize that because of temperament some people have a much more difficult problem on their hands than others. Imaginative and sensitive people, for example, are likely to be more subject to moods than the tougher type, who are not much affected by what is going on around them.

To some extent moods may be caused by our state of health. Depression and irritability may be due to nothing more nor less than tiredness. Rest can put that right. Most tiredness actually arises in the mind even when it is felt in the body. Monotony, leading to boredom, easily causes depression or irritability, and many a wife, when housework and mending have 'got her down', could be quickly cured by an outing.

Again, moods may be the result of conflicts going on in the unconscious mind. We don't know what is the matter, but we feel depressed and miserable. Pretty nearly everybody knows that experience, because we have all got a few unconscious conflicts tucked away. Occasional gloomy moods, then, are nothing more than our common human lot, but, if they are extreme or persist so that we cannot shake them off, we shall be wise to go to a good psychologist and find out what the trouble is.

Women have the reputation of being more moody than men. Poets have had a good deal to say about the fickleness of the fair sex and the torments they inflict upon their lovers, all of whom are, presumably, like Caesar, 'constant as the northern star', and not in the least subject to unpredictable moods. Like every generalization of the kind, that is only a half-truth. There are men as moody as any woman. But it is true that the great majority of women are, to some extent, affected by their monthly cycle—a factor which men have not to contend with. There is a certain amount of glandular upset, sometimes accompanied by feelings of depression. Many of them, too, experience some pain or discomfort, and that is apt, naturally, to produce irritability. Men ought to be understanding and considerate, and certainly should not regard them as weak creatures. It is probably true (another generalization!) that, on the whole, women bear pain and discomfort with more fortitude than we do. If we had to look forward to a few days of pain, inconvenience or gloom every month with dreadful regularity, we should probably become quite insufferable.

There is another way in which the monthly cycle affects the moods of most women—and possibly this was what took the bloom off last Saturday. There is a periodic variation in the strength of their sexual desire. In the majority, it is strongest a few days before the period and again a few days after it is over. (That does not mean it may not arise spontaneously or cannot be aroused at other times.) Perhaps Jill was at a point in the rhythm when sex feeling was low, and, therefore, she did not respond as ardently as usual to your love-making. At such times a man, who doesn't understand, is apt to think that a girl is just being perverse in order to annoy or put him to some sort of test. He demands to know what he has done to deserve this coldness. Presently, if he is foolish enough, he is reproaching the poor girl with ceasing to care for him or even with having found another lover. There you have the makings of a first-class row! She protests tearfully that she does love him, and perhaps doesn't understand any more than he does why she does not feel as ardent as she did the last time they were out together.

Even after marriage some men don't manage to grasp this bit of feminine psychology, and are disgruntled or worse if their wives don't always respond with enthusiasm to their advances.

Well, I hope both you and Jill have emerged from the passing cloud which blotted out the sun last Saturday and made you both feel distinctly chilly. I've little doubt about it. I hope something in this letter may give you a line on the matter. Anyway, don't ever forget that moods are queer things, which we should try to understand, and which we should not treat too seriously.

VIII

Getting a sound attitude to sex

I QUITE agree with you that it's time 'we got down to the whole business of sex'. But I don't much like that way of putting it. Probably you didn't mean it so, but it seems to suggest that you're thinking, 'Somehow I shall have to come to terms with it, but it's a bit of a nuisance. That's where the real snags of marriage are, and, if it weren't for that, everything would be a lot simpler.' Now, it's perfectly true that sex is responsible for a great many difficulties and not a few tragedies. It can make men and women downright cruel to one another, and I'm not surprised that some people curse sex and everything to do with it. But that does not mean that in itself it is an evil thing. The truth is that sex, like everything which nature has put into us, is neither good nor bad; it all depends on the use we make of it. So many of our troubles come from the *mis*-use of things which have wonderful possibilities of happiness and good. Well, that's how it is with sex. It does cause people—a lot of people—a great deal of trouble and misery because for some reason it is mishandled. But it opens out to men and women possibilities of a full and complete life, which could not be realized if they were without all that we ought to mean by the word 'sex'. A man and woman who were entirely devoid of sexual feelings for each other (or for anybody else) might achieve a happy and harmonious life together—so far as it went. But it simply wouldn't hold the same possibilities of happiness and satisfaction as are open to a pair of married lovers. Things might in some ways be simpler for the sexless couple, but there is a whole range and depth of life which they could never experience, and which they wouldn't be able to understand in the least if you talked to them about it.

I remember the first time a man came and told me he was going to get married and wanted me to talk to him. I said 'All right. Where do you want me to start?' 'Well', he said, 'you know I work at X's. There are hundreds of chaps there, and I've got a pair of ears, so I've heard a thing or two. But I'm not sure that I know anything accurately—scientifically, if you see what I mean. So I guess you'd better start right at the beginning.' That seemed to me sensible enough, and I got down to it on the spot. I was young then, and I thought the first thing to do was to set him up with all the knowledge he ought to have about the make-up of his own body and his wife's. Of course, that was perfectly sound. But it wasn't the right place to begin, because, you see, a man (or a woman) might be a professor of anatomy and yet fail completely to achieve a satisfactory sex life. We'll come back to physiology later on. We'll call a spade a spade, and we'll go into the question in sufficient detail for all practical purposes. The first thing to be done is to make sure that Jill and you have a sound *attitude* to sex. If you have, the getting of the necessary knowledge is as easy as falling off a log.

Crowds of people, both men and women, have the idea that there is something about sex which isn't 'quite nice'. That's putting it mildly. Some (especially women) think it's beastly. That devastating notion may have been implanted in them in a thousand different ways. Let me give you a few examples. A mother has had an unfortunate sex life. Perhaps she is tied up to a husband who really has made sex a beastly thing. In that miserable situation (like many other mothers) she confides something of her troubles to a daughter who is still a mere child and cannot check up on what she is told. So, of course, the girl believes it, and what she is told in early days by her own mother, with obvious disgust and loathing, sinks deep. Or a girl overhears women saying what they think about some man (who may quite possibly deserve it all), and she supposes, when she has heard that sort of thing a few times, that all men are beasts. Or she comes into a room where grown-ups are talking, and there are hasty sounds of 'Sh! Sh!' accompanied with knowing smiles and clumsily engineered attempts to change the subject. But she has heard enough to know that they are talking about babies and the mysterious goings-on between men and women, so she concludes there is something in all this which can't be decently talked about. Possibly some man interferes with the sex organs of a little boy or girl, or in some other way causes a shock or 'trauma', as the psychologists call it. Very likely the child tells nobody, but drives the terrifying memory down into the unconscious mind, where it generates an anxiety which shows itself in everything to do with sex. Perhaps a boy is found to be masturbating (i.e. handling his penis or somehow contriving to excite it), and is threatened by a parent or some other stupid adult with all sorts of terrible things. Sometimes a girl is not prepared by explanations for the onset of menstruation, and is horrified and afraid. A woman told me once that she used to creep along back streets during her periods because she thought everybody must know about it and think her unclean, and she had never got over the feeling. A boy may have the same sort of shock if he is not told beforehand about the nocturnal emissions of semen which will begin at puberty. Or a child may happen to see (if he sleeps in the same room) or overhear (if he sleeps in another) an act of intercourse between the parents and is scared, thinking that father is hurting mother.

That's enough to illustrate my point that disgust and fear may arise in all sorts of ways. Now, if Jill or you should happen to feel that way at all, you simply must do everything which can be done to get straightened out before you marry. If it happens to be some superficial difficulty, the kind of thing I shall be able to say in these letters may clear it up, but if it has deeper roots let me beg and beseech you, as you value your happiness, to go to a psychologist and let him find out where the trouble really lies. Talk it all out with Jill straight away, and make sure you can both give the 'All clear!' It is a dreadful situation when these things are never mentioned, and, after they are married, a husband or wife suddenly reveals a hatred or fear of sex.

Now, there are a lot of other people who would not say they loathe the whole idea of sex, and yet they are not entirely reconciled to it. As they see it, sex is something which has to be accepted and tolerated up to a point, but in the back of the mind, at any rate, there is the thought that it really belongs to their 'lower nature'. It is something which, as a concession to human weakness, must be tolerated and even gratified up to a point in the privacy of the bedroom, but it's really a rather shameful episode! And it must be rigidly segregated from all the respectable and presentable parts of life. After all, it's an affair of *bodies!* It brings us down to the level of the animals. Man's proper life is on a higher plane altogether. Intellectual and 'refined' people are rather given to this kind of attitude, and sometimes wrong-headed religious teaching helps to create it. People have quite mistaken notions as to what the New Testament means by 'the flesh', of which it obviously has a poor opinion! The New Testament is pretty severe on abuses of sex (though it's much harder on many other things), but it does not suggest that sex in itself is evil. Jesus certainly never did.

Well, there isn't much hope of a happy and satisfying sexual adjustment if a couple think that their nice, respectable life is lived in the sitting-room, the dining-room and the kitchen, while the indecencies (!) of sex must be tolerated in the bedroom. There is bound to be strain and tension when any part of the personality is not integrated into the rest in such a way that life moves as one whole piece. You see, it is not enough just to tolerate sex because we can't get rid of it. (Some people do try to get rid of it by repressing it—i.e. pushing it down into the unconscious mind and pretending it isn't there. Then the trouble begins in earnest, for that way lie nervous breakdowns and all sorts of complications.) It must be accepted as something which is normal and healthy. It must be welcomed with both hands as a gift of nature full of tremendous possibilities for those who will learn how to use it. Yes, *learn!* More about that later.

If sex is to mean what it can and ought to mean in your marriage, you must begin with the realization that the spiritual and physical can't be separated. It is possible, of course, to treat sex as a purely physical thing, and plenty of people do. In other words, they use another person's body as a means of relieving a physical tension, as a man does when he goes to a prostitute or as a woman does when she 'picks up' a man. Sexual intercourse is then not much different from the copulation of animals. There is no real *personal relationship* involved. But sexual communion between married lovers can be the complete expression through their bodies of the union of their personalities—an expression so intimate that it never loses its wonder however often they have enjoyed it. When people relieve a physical tension with some chance acquaintance, they often feel contempt and disgust for their 'partners' as soon as desire is sated. But when two married lovers express in that way the union they already feel, they experience an indescribable nearness and a sense of peace and balance throughout every part of their lives. Perhaps I have made it seem as though sexual intercourse is a sort of terminus, an expression of a perfect companionship which already exists. And so it can be. But it would be equally true to think of it as a thoroughfare—as a way by which two lovers, trying to reach complete companionship, are helped towards it. If they don't achieve sexual harmony because of inhibitions in one or both of them, or because their knowledge and technique are faulty, their progress towards a perfectly satisfying life together may be seriously retarded. For the more they love each other the more they will feel the need of the complete and mutual expression which nature has made possible through sex. If they do not achieve it, irritation and nervous strain may undermine the life of companionship they are trying to build up together. So it will be worth while for Jill and you to go to any amount of trouble to get your sex life right. You may be one of the lucky couples for whom everything is perfectly plain sailing from the start. If you do come up against some difficulties, patience and knowledge will probably enable you to overcome them. Since sex is a gift of nature it might seem that the light of nature would be a safe and adequate guide in the sex life. But it isn't. It appears to me that nature doesn't teach men and women much more than how to beget children. It leaves them pretty much in the dark as to how they can help each other to achieve a satisfying sex life.

IX

The sex organs

IN order to manage a motor-car successfully you don't need a detailed knowledge of the structure and composition of every single bit of it. There's a lot of technical stuff which matters only to the specialist, and you can drive your car quite happily and without getting your licence endorsed if you have a minimum of knowledge—provided you do know the right things and that you know them accurately. You must be sound on the functions of the parts which are involved in driving, and you must be able to tell if something isn't working properly, so that you can get expert help if necessary. It's like that with sex. You don't need to bother your head with all the information contained in massive medical text-books, but you do need to know enough about the form and function of the organs of both sexes to be sure that you can use them aright in your married life. A lot of people have vague ideas and that's about all, so I think, as my friend said, we had better start from the beginning.

From the biological point of view the object of sexual union is the bringing of a male seed into contact with a female egg so that the two can fuse together and form a new life.

The male seeds (or sperms) are manufactured in two organs called the testicles. These are oval in shape, about an inch and a half long and an inch or so wide and they hang in the pouch of skin (called the scrotum) where the legs join. In these two factories, which work from the time a boy reaches puberty, millions and millions of sperms are made. In the act of sexual intercourse the sperms are ejaculated, millions at a time, in a milky fluid manufactured by other glands. A sperm is a microscopic organism, about one five-hundredth of an inch in length, and under a microscope would look something like a tadpole. It has a sort of tail by which it is able to swim along in the moisture of the female organs, so that it can find its way into the womb (or uterus), and there fuse with the egg (ovum). When the ejaculation is about to take place, this seminal fluid passes into the urethra—the passage by which water is excreted from the bladder, and which runs along the whole length of the penis.

The penis is an organ several inches in length which hangs down in front of the scrotum. Under the stimulus of sexual excitement the penis becomes erect, i.e. it increases greatly in size, stiffens and stands out from the body. This erection has to take place before it can penetrate into the female organs. The top of the penis is called the glans. It is covered with exceedingly sensitive skin, and when it is sufficiently stimulated by contact with the female organs, ejaculation of the semen takes place. This ejaculation is brought about by reflex action, i.e. by muscular movements which can't be controlled by the will.

The female sex organs are much more inside the body. Indeed, all that can be seen of them is the labia majora (greater lips). These are the two fleshy folds between the legs. Inside them are the labia minora (lesser lips), which are sensitive to stimulation.

Where these inner lips join there is a small organ called the clitoris. It has no function in the sexual or reproductive processes except to provide sensation. Like the penis, it becomes erect under the stimulation of touch or as the result of sexual excitement, and it is then about as big as a pea. A great many nerves are centred in this little organ, and from it sensations spread to other parts.

Inside the inner lips is the entrance to the vagina, which is the passage leading to the womb. The word vagina means 'sheath', and the passage is so called because it is like a sheath into which the penis fits. At the entrance to the vagina there is a thin membrane called the hymen, which partially closes the passage. It used to be thought that if a woman did not have the hymen intact it was a proof that she had had intercourse before marriage, and many brides have been cruelly and unjustly accused by suspicious husbands. It is now generally agreed by doctors that the hymen may be absent at birth or may be broken in a number of ways, which do not in the least indicate unchastity. The hymen, when it *is* intact, resists the entrance of the penis, and, if a husband is rough or impatient, the membrane may be torn away from the walls of the passage, causing some pain and bleeding. In some cases it is so thickened that it needs to be stretched by a doctor.

Just inside the vagina are two little glands, one on each side. They are called Bartholin's glands, and their job is to provide a lubricating fluid, which makes it possible for the penis to penetrate easily. They provide enough lubrication only under the stimulation of sexual excitement. The friction of the penis in the vagina causes sensations which, sometimes in conjunction with those centred in the clitoris, cause the muscular walls to contract rhythmically when they have been sufficiently stimulated.

The vagina, which is about four inches long, leads up to the womb. This is the place where the baby lives and grows until it finds its way into the world via the vagina. The womb is pear-shaped, about three and a half inches by two, and the walls, which are made of muscle, are an inch thick. The womb is able to expand tremendously as the baby grows, and these muscles help to launch it on its journey to the outside world. The thin end of the pear-shaped womb projects into the top of the vagina. It is called the neck of the womb (cervix), and has a tiny opening through which the sperm can enter in search of the egg.

The eggs are made in two factories corresponding to the testicles in the male. They are the ovaries, which are situated on the right and left of the womb, and they are connected with the upper end of it by the Fallopian tubes, which are about five and a half inches long. In each ovary there are thousands of egg cells, each about one three-hundredth of an inch long. Every month one emerges and is passed along the tubes by muscular movements. If it happens to meet a sperm and fuse with it, conception takes place, the fertilized egg embeds itself in the walls of the womb, and the baby begins to grow. If it does not encounter a sperm, it just passes through the womb and away via the vagina. When the egg is released from the ovary, the womb prepares a special lining for its reception if it should be fertilized. If that doesn't happen and the lining is not needed, the cells which compose it disintegrate and pass out through the vagina with a certain amount of blood and other secretions. This is called menstruation, and you can see why the non-appearance of the monthly period may be a sign that a baby is on the way.

Well, that's the end of the anatomy lecture! Simple, isn't it? But, as I told you, knowledge of anatomy by itself won't get you far. You have to know the art of making love so that body responds to mind and spirit.

Making sure you're fit

SOME time (and the sooner the better) I think both Jill and you should go to a doctor and get overhauled. It is sometimes argued that a couple should not be allowed to marry without obtaining certificates of medical fitness. I shouldn't like to see that made compulsory, but I think a couple owe it to each other (not to mention the children who may be born) to take the question of physical health seriously.

Ideally they should have a medical examination shortly before they get engaged. If the engagement comes about by easy stages, that is quite practicable. Sometimes, however, it is all rather sudden. Even if the couple have known each other for a longish time, the possibility of marriage may not have been mentioned. If, then, the ardent lover should clasp his beloved and whisper, 'Will you be my wife?' and she should reply, 'This is rather sudden, but the answer is "Yes—subject to satisfactory medical reports",' the whole thing would be rather dispiriting. But there would be some common sense in the answer all the same.

The primary object of a pre-marriage medical examination is to ascertain that the general state of health is sound. Take an obvious example. If one of the partners is unsuspectingly suffering from tuberculosis or some other serious disease, it is right that both should know it. (If there is the least possibility of venereal disease in either partner, an examination is essential, and the marriage should not take place until there is a clean bill of health; otherwise there may be disaster for the other partner and for the children.) I am not saying that, even if something serious is discovered, the engagement ought necessarily to be called off. I have known marriages which turned out happily even when one of the parties suffered from some grave disability. But I think people should enter into marriage with their eyes wide open. A couple ought to take such facts into consideration, and ask how they are likely to react on the marriage, and whether they affect the question of having children.

It is sometimes said that a couple should be examined with a view to ascertaining whether their union will prove fertile, because that would help to avoid the disappointment of the childless marriage. There have no doubt been many cases in which the failure to have a family has been a cause of bitterness, and, had a couple known that their union would prove sterile, they perhaps would not have married. (Incidentally, it used to be the wife who always got the blame if no baby arrived, and barrenness was regarded as a reproach. It is now known that it may just as likely be the man who is sterile, and, in any case, sterility is a misfortune, not a fault.)

Well, on the principle I have just set down—that a couple should go into marriage with their eyes open to their physical handicaps, if there are any—you may say, 'Then it's surely wise to be tested for fertility.'

But it's not just as simple as that. The ordinary medical man would be able to detect any obvious malformation in either of you which would prevent your having children, but an examination really worth while would require tests which he would not be in a position to carry out. Even if you went to a specialist, he probably wouldn't be able to give you anything like certainty. You see, a woman might show every sign that she would be fertile, and a man might have any number of active sperms in his semen, yet they might never have a child, though both of them might have had as many as the old woman who lived in a shoe if they had mated with other partners. Or—to take a very different situation—a man may not be producing any sperms at all when he is examined, and even a number of examinations may return a negative result. But perhaps now and again he *may* produce a few—and with luck, remember, even one might lead to conception. Therefore, a doctor who told him positively that he would *never* beget a child would be rather rash. My point is that there isn't any certainty. If there is any gross malformation in either of the partners that's another story, and the couple ought to know about it before they marry. Otherwise, it seems to me, it is better to leave the future to settle the question of fertility. If, after a time, a baby does not begin to come, by all means seek expert advice and don't delay too long, for in these days medical science can help in many cases. And, if a child never does come, you must never hand out blame, but help each other to get over the disappointment and find other outlets for the love and care you would so gladly have given him.

When Jill has her medical examination, she should ask the doctor about the hymen. If it is thickened and tough, so that union would be painful at first, she should go to him again a few weeks before your wedding so that he can stretch it. Among many primitive peoples the hymen is removed, as a preparation for marriage, in the initiation ceremonies which mark a girl's entry into womanhood. Some girls (probably the great majority) in this country don't have the matter investigated and, if necessary, attended to, out of false modesty or just because it's too much trouble. Then on the honeymoon intercourse may prove painful—perhaps so painful that it is impossible. When they return home they hurry off to the doctor. But marriage has begun in disappointment—which is a pity when the trouble could so easily have been averted.

XI

The art of making love

THERE are a good many terms for sexual union, and I suppose names don't matter much. But there is one I rather dislike, because it is misleading if you take it as any more than a mere label. I mean 'the sex act'. That suggests it is an action, like brushing your teeth, which begins at a certain moment, lasts for a few seconds or a few minutes, and comes to an abrupt end, so that you could time it with a stop-watch. It's an isolated action, if you see what I mean, which has no relation to what goes before or comes after. And, in point of fact, that is exactly what it is for a lot of couples, and it is exactly what it ought not to be. You can't say when a real experience of sexual communion begins and ends.

A wife said to me bitterly some time ago, 'He asks for it just as if he were asking for a cup of tea. What's the use of that? It means nothing to me.' That's just what would be said by a lot of women who are indifferent to the physical side of marriage or who positively loathe it. Any number of men set about intercourse in the most matter-of-fact sort of way with or without asking. They say in effect, 'I want to relieve a sexual urge. Here's my wife. That's what she's here for. So here goes!' Often the wife takes it as a matter of course, too. She has never got any pleasure out of it, doesn't expect any, perhaps doesn't even know there's any to be had. Therefore, as she sees the matter, it's something to be gone through with, and the sooner it's begun the sooner it will be over. There are other men whose attitude to the sexual relationship is quite different, inasmuch as they honestly do want it to mean something to their wives, and yet they go about it in much the same way because they don't understand either the physical or psychological make-up of a woman. For them, too, it is an *act* with a definite beginning and end.

Now, I've said already that the very essence of a successful sex life is freedom and spontaneity. So it may happen now and again with some couples, at any rate, that they will suddenly fling themselves into each other's arms and consummate their love without having known two minutes before that it would happen. Some sudden stimulus or uprush of mutual passion has drawn them to each other at the same moment. That is pretty much a matter of temperament; it would never happen to some people. If the urge comes like that it is a good thing if love can have its way. In that case the wife reaches in a flash the point of desire at which she is prepared for union.

But if Jill happens to be the kind of girl in whom passion can suddenly rise to such intensity, that won't be usual even in her case. You must remember a fundamental difference between man and woman. A man in a twinkling, because of some powerful stimulus to his emotions, may be psychologically and physically ready for union, but it generally takes a woman a considerable time to reach that height of desire. If she isn't ready, intercourse won't give her any pleasure. In fact, if she isn't psychologically ready she won't be physically ready either. Her desire must be aroused before her glands lubricate her organs so that the penis can enter easily, and, if she is not prepared in that way, she may actually be hurt if her husband persists in going on.

The point I am driving at (and I don't apologize for sticking to it, because it is so often forgotten) is that a complete experience of sexual union requires preparation. It is nearly always essential for a woman. And so it is for a man if it is to be *complete*, for while he may 'start from cold' and get a physical climax in a few minutes, that is not all that sexual union can mean for him. Indeed, some men would say that the physical sensations of sex, apart from the psychological and spiritual experience of union with a beloved woman, are not so very wonderful.

The ideal sexual union follows as a natural sequel to an experience of mental and spiritual nearness. It may follow a long and understanding talk, an evening's reading by the fire, a visit to a concert or theatre, a country walk, a job of work or service which has been done together—in fact, it may be the consummation of a nearness which has come through *sharing* something together. Many married lovers would say that under such conditions they have had their most satisfying unions. It isn't to be expected that a husband and wife will always feel as near to each other as on those occasions when something has drawn them specially close, but, if the union of their bodies is not the expression of some degree of harmony already existing, it is emptied of most of its meaning. It may sometimes draw them close when, for some reason, they are not feeling as near each other as usual, but that is because the *desire* to be in complete harmony is there.

I have been saying that intercourse between husband and wife has as its goal something very much more than the production of certain physical sensations in the two partners. All the same, those physical effects must be secured, for otherwise the union, so far from consummating the sense of nearness or helping to produce it, will make the husband and wife feel farther away from each other. And in order to produce the physical sensations which will culminate in mutual orgasm (I'll say something about that later), a technique of love-making has to be mastered. That includes a way of preparing for union and also a technique of coitus which is the name for the 'sex act'. In this letter I am only talking about the preliminaries.

If a husband is going to be a successful lover, he simply must realize that there are two differences between his make-up and his wife's.

The first is that, except on those rare occasions when a woman is swept away by a sudden gust of passion, she has to be courted and wooed before she is physically and mentally ready for union. And that must be a gradual process. It's useless to try to rush it. A woman wants to be talked to when she lies in her husband's arms. Many men are not specially good at that. They are apt to be tongue-tied and to lack imagination. That sort of thing, they say, may be all right for poets, but we're not poets, and, anyhow, we've said it all before! It would certainly be hard on a man if his wife expected him never to repeat himself from his marriage day to his golden wedding! Fortunately the majority of women are not so exacting. Of course, they like variety and imagination, but they are ready to hear the same things over and over again so long as they are sure they are not just words, but *mean* something. I heard a wife say, when she was getting near her golden wedding, 'He still

says the things he used to say—but they mean so much more now.'
I suppose the people who always have to be dashing off after some
new sexual adventure would tear their hair at the thought of such
boredom, but that would only be because they simply could not
understand what she meant when she said, '*they mean so much
more now*'.

And a wife likes to be looked at. Eyes speak as well as lips—often
much more eloquently. Many a wife will respond when a husband
bends over her and gazes into her eyes much more quickly than
she would to any amount of more direct sexual stimulation. If she
is as free from inhibitions as she ought to be, she will like him to
gaze at her whole body—not with the lascivious eye of a roué, but
with the eyes of a lover who never loses his reverence. It means a
lot to a woman to know that her husband thinks her body is
beautiful and that he is emotionally moved by it. (Of course, it will
mean still more to her when she gets older and fears she is losing
her physical charms.)

The second thing a man must remember is that sexual sensations are widely diffused throughout a woman's body, whereas in
his own they are pretty well confined to the sex organs. There are
some parts which are particularly sensitive—e.g. the lips, the
breasts (especially the nipples) and the neck. Naturally, the degree
of sensitiveness of the various regions of the body may vary somewhat in different women. If Jill and you are as frank with each
other as you ought to be, she will tell you where the most sensitive
spots are and what kind of stimulation gives her most pleasure.
As a woman becomes sexually aroused the whole body grows
sensitive and the understanding husband so conducts his love-
making that he gradually increases her desire. His kisses will vary
from the light brushing of her lips to the passionate kiss. Only
gradually, having caressed the other parts of his wife's body
which give her pleasure, will he approach the direct stimulation of
the sexual organs. At first he will stroke the labia and clitoris
lightly and move his hand away again to the thighs or some other
part of the body, until she gradually desires the more intense
stimulation of the sex organs. At this stage of love-making there
must be no breaking-off. Their bodies are drawn together in ever
closer contact in preparation for the final union.

I have been talking so far about the husband's part in love-making, but you must not run away with the idea that the wife is to be merely passive. She must not simply return kisses and caresses; she must sometimes take the initiative. From the physical point of view she has less scope because, as I pointed out, a man's sensations are more localized, and too much stimulation of his sexual organs may cause a premature ejaculation and make union impossible. By taking an active part a wife facilitaties the arousing of her own desire. She must not be held back by inhibitions or false ideas about modesty. A husband likes to see the rising tide of passion in his wife. Of course he does. He knows that he is then more likely to give her satisfaction and he knows, too, that he is loved, for precious few wives would *make* love to their husbands if they did not really love them.

All these preludes to physical union are sometimes called 'love play', which is an excellent name for them because it suggests the freedom and spontaneity which, as I keep on saying, is the essence of satisfying sex life. A healthy-minded couple of married lovers can do whatever mood or fancy suggests to increase their mutual desire and pleasure in each other. Why not?

XII

Orgasm and 'technique'

I PROMISED in a previous letter that I would say something about orgasm and the technique of coitus. So let's get down to it.

I find that a lot of couples who are going to get married, and many who have been married for years, have never heard of orgasm. That wouldn't matter if they only knew about what it stands for—what's in a name, anyway?—but they don't. Orgasm means the climax of sexual excitement in *both* sexes. There isn't much mystery about it in the case of a man. It means the ejaculation of the seminal fluid, when the stimulation of the penis has reached a point at which it is brought about by reflex (i.e. involuntary) muscular movements. But what neither the man nor the woman knows in many cases is that the wife should reach an equally definite climax. What precisely happens in a woman's orgasm is not so easy to describe, partly because it is much more complicated, and partly because it varies a good deal from one woman to another. Here is a description given me by a woman who had, by the way, been married for twelve years before she experienced orgasm at all. Sexual excitement, she says, is 'a feeling of inward stirrings rather than anything else', and, when the moment of intercourse approaches this becomes 'an actual movement in the vaginal region—a sort of rhythmic motion. . . . This movement is intensified during stimulation (of the clitoris), which gives rise to other sensations. These tend to subside when penetration takes place, but the vaginal movement continues. I must describe here my mental attitude during all this. I feel as if I am floating away—as if nothing else matters except this intense feeling of pleasure, until, with the climax, internal sensations seem to work up to boiling point and spread all over the body, when I cease floating and seem to awake out of a dream in a somewhat breathless condition.'

That is a description of a very complete orgasm, and the intensity of the experience would vary in different women. Some, for example, have quite strong rhythmic muscular contractions lasting from twelve to fifteen or even twenty seconds, others find that the movements are scarcely perceptible. The crux of the matter is, in any case, that the woman should feel a steadily mounting sexual excitement, which reaches a climax and then subsides. It should perhaps be added that some women are capable of more than one orgasm if intercourse is prolonged.

Now, the immediate aim of sexual intercourse is to produce the orgasm simultaneously in both partners. That may not be easy to achieve at first, and may call for a good deal of acquired skill in love-making. The difficulty often is that the man's orgasm comes before the woman has reached hers, and, in order to avoid that, the skilful management of their minds and bodies is necessary and frequently has to be learned.

Most important is the love-play, which should neither be omitted nor hurried, except on those rare occasions when mutual desire is overpowering. The stage of love-play ends with the introduction of the fully erect penis into the vagina. It is unwise to attempt to make connexion until it is *fully* erect, otherwise ejaculation is likely to occur at once.

Now, the question of position is of some importance. Several things have to be borne in mind in determining what position is best: the comfort and freedom from strain of both partners; the need to secure the greatest possible stimulation of the clitoris and the vagina; and the utmost freedom of movement for both.

For some reason it seems to be generally assumed in this country that there is only one 'proper' position, viz., that in which the wife is lying on her back with the husband on top of her. It does not occur to a great many people that any other arrangement is possible. Yet some races habitually adopt different positions and take a very poor view of that which has become conventional among us. Theoretically, in this position the clitoris is stimulated by the movements of the penis so that sensation is secured in the vagina and the clitoris at the same time, which is certainly very desirable if not always absolutely essential to the wife's orgasm. In actual fact many women do not feel any stimulation of the clitoris in that position, and it has obvious disadvantages—the wife may feel oppressed by the weight of her husband's body, especially if he happens to be heavy and does not properly support himself with his arms; she has practically no freedom of movement; and frequently there is not very deep penetration of the vagina. In some cases a pillow placed under the wife's hips will help to adjust the angle of the vagina to the penis.

A position which has a great deal to recommend it, at least as an occasional variation, is that in which the husband lies on his back and the wife sits astride him. Connexion is easily made in this attitude and penetration is complete. The husband cannot move much, but the wife has complete freedom, and by bending the body forwards or backwards she can find the positions which produce most sensation.

Sometimes the husband lies behind the wife. In this position, also, his hands are free to caress her body, but for some couples the position would be impracticable.

Another variation is the side-by-side position. If the legs are in any way interlocked the possibilities of movement are limited for both partners. If, however, the wife separates her legs, drawing up the one, which is underneath, until it is about at a right-angle with her body, and the husband lies between them, it is in many ways the most satisfactory of all positions. There is no pressure on the wife, both have freedom of movement, there is complete penetration, and the husband can, if so desired, stimulate the clitoris with his fingers during intercourse.

There are, of course, many other possible positions, which married lovers can discover for themselves. They should never let themselves fall into a routine so that intercourse is *always* carried through in the same way and in the same position. Remember the vital importance of spontaneity and variety in love-making. By experiment and mutual helpfulness every couple must discover for themselves what best meets their physical and psychological needs.

Especially in the early days of marriage the achievement of connexion may present some little difficulty. Things are simplified a great deal when the wife uses her hands to direct the penis into the vagina. Some women do not take this common-sense step because of false modesty, some because they think that, if their husbands were any sort of men, it wouldn't be necessary, and some because it just doesn't occur to them. Wives could quite easily save themselves discomfort and even pain, and spare both themselves and their husbands a good deal of irritation at what looks like clumsiness, but is not necessarily anything of the sort.

An additional little complication is sometimes caused by the insufficient lubrication of the vagina, though that will not often be the case if the love-play has been adequate. A little artificial lubrication will soon get over the difficulty. A more serious obstacle is a contraction of the muscles, which closes the vagina at the moment when union is about to take place. If that continues to happen the wife should go to her doctor, who may find that she needs the services of a psychologist. The trouble is not frequent, but is liable to occur especially when a bride has been clumsily or brutally treated by her husband in his first approaches. It is obviously a method of self-defence, and in such cases the husband may need help and advice as much as the wife.

When union has been effected, it is sometimes wise for the couple to lie still for a little while. The act of penetration is likely to stimulate the penis a great deal and further movement at once might cause premature ejaculation. When the husband feels that the nerves of the penis have settled down the two partners can begin to move slowly, gently and rhythmically, pressing together at the same time. The tempo will be gradually increased, but the rhythm must not be broken. Some couples find that, if the husband's ejaculation seems imminent and the wife is not approaching orgasm, it is a good thing to lie still for a few moments and then to begin again, but this cessation of movement would lessen the possibility of orgasm for some women. Here, again, every couple must discover for themselves what technique suits them best. Certainly the needs of the wife should be the chief factor in deciding the tempo of the rhythm and the rate of its increase. The husband must try to control his own reactions so that he does not reach his orgasm too quickly. It will help him to do this if he concentrates his thoughts on his wife's reactions rather than his own. Sometimes the advice is given that he should turn his thoughts to other matters altogether. That may be all right up to a point, but some men do it so effectively that they seem to their wives to have lost interest in the love-making, with the result that their sensations, too, die down. Ideally, the vigour and rhythm of motion should steadily increase without interruption, and the passion and sensations of both should rise together, so that they reach orgasm at the same moment. Often it is, in fact, the muscular contractions of the penis at the moment of ejaculation which provide the final stimulus for the wife and induce her orgasm.

What I have been describing is what ought ideally to happen. Unfortunately it doesn't always. Often the wife is not near orgasm when the husband's ejaculation occurs, but his erection then subsides and she can receive little further stimulation. The number of wives who *always* reach orgasm is probably quite a small minority. It is estimated that about one in three never or very seldom achieves it. Many more could have satisfaction, at any rate sometimes, if their husbands were really concerned that they should. No words of condemnation are too strong for the selfish fellow who does not *care* whether his wife gets satisfaction or not so long as he has what he wants.

If ejaculation has happened too quickly for the wife to reach her climax, the husband may soon be able to resume intercourse. Some men can achieve another erection quickly; some can't. If that is impossible orgasm may be induced if stimulation of the clitoris is continued. At any rate, every husband should do what he can to give his wife satisfaction. Continual excitement with no sort of relief is a pretty wearying business, and is a prime cause of a great many of the irritations and bothers of married life.

One last word on this subject—and it is especially for Jill. If you are not satisfied and are not securing a proper orgasm, for goodness' sake don't pretend that you are. Some women do—and with the best and kindest of motives. They think their husbands would be so disappointed if they knew satisfaction hadn't come, and they hope things will soon turn out all right so that they won't have to pretend any more. But they may be unlucky. Then they get themselves into a complete jam. They daren't reveal how things really are, because they think that, after having been 'deceived' for so long, their husbands may be angry, despairing or humiliated. And so they keep up the pitiful pretence, while they grow to dislike the whole sex life more and more until, perhaps to the utter bewilderment of their husbands, the whole story one day comes out in a flood of tears. Remember, then, frankness and confidence must be the rule here as in every other part of married life. If that obtains, you can face your difficulties together and see what can be done about them.

XIII

Why orgasm is not achieved

YES, I agree with you that it's a bit tough that so few couples reach orgasm together and that so many women never experience it at all. But I'm not sure that you're so right in blaming Nature for 'making a hash of it'. Anthropologists tell us that the primitive races seem to have no difficulty in achieving the physical satisfaction of sex. That's not because they are promiscuous. As a matter of fact, many 'savage' races have much more rigid standards of chastity than we have in these days. It is because among them there is nothing 'hush-hush' about sex, and so they are taught what there is to know. They haven't had a lot of inhibitions clamped down on them, and they are not emotionally dammed up as so many of us are. So it looks as though 'civilization' is more to blame than 'Nature'. Only in very rare cases is a person born with a physical defect which makes orgasm impossible, and we are not born with a psychological defect either. The trouble lies in the wrong ideas and emotional attitudes which we somehow pick up or have thrust upon us. Suppose we have a look at some of the causes.

When a couple cannot have mutual orgasm the difficulty may be in the man, in the woman, or in both.

Take first the difficulties which bother men. Of course, all men, whether they have relations with the other sex or not, have orgasm sometimes. If the discharge of the accumulated seminal fluid is not brought about in some other way, erections and emissions will occur in sleep, probably during some kind of erotic dream. But some men cannot achieve orgasm with a woman, and others, while they can bring about their own, cannot enable their partners to reach theirs. That is generally due to one of two reasons: either they cannot secure an erection at all and so cannot even begin intercourse, or else ejaculation takes place so quickly that (as I said in the last letter) the woman can't achieve her climax in time.

Now, when a man who is physically normal cannot secure an erection, obviously there is some complete inhibition at work. If for some reason he consciously does not want to have intercourse, there is nothing very surprising about it, but sometimes a husband wants union desperately and yet is completely impotent. In that case something in his *unconscious* mind is saying: 'You must not have intercourse'—it may be with *any* woman or perhaps only with *this* woman.

There may be dozens of reasons for that. The man may be homosexual—i.e. his desires may be towards his own sex and not the other. There is, of course, a homosexual element in us which is normal. It is especially strong round about adolescence and accounts for 'pashes' and 'crushes'—but we ought to outgrow it. Some men with strong homosexual tendencies are capable of intercourse, but some are not. No man with such homosexual desires ought to marry until a psychologist has straightened him out. Some, unfortunately, do marry, thinking that, when they are in the new and intimate relationship with their wives, 'things will right themselves'—which they won't.

Some men, because of a sexual shock in childhood or because of bad teaching (or none), get a wrong attitude to sex, as I was saying in an earlier letter. Therefore, when the time comes for them to use their sexual powers, they can't do it because of their horror or fear of sex. Something in their conscious, or more likely their unconscious, mind is saying, 'You mustn't have anything to do with such a dreadful or nasty thing.'

The bogy of masturbation frightens some men into impotence. They have been told it is a terrible vice which lands people in asylums. (Yes, such things are still said!) So, even if they gave up masturbation long ago, they think the habit did them some irreparable damage, which has made them unable to fulfil their sexual function properly. The fact is, of course, that masturbation would have to be excessive to a degree before it did any physical harm. What amount of psychological harm it does depends on the strength of the guilty feeling attached to it and on the reason for the habit in any given case. Masturbation in childhood and adolescence is simply a kind of exploration. If it persists, it is probably a symptom of failure to secure adjustment in personal relationships, and the relationship to lover or wife will probably only be one aspect of the total situation. Anyway, masturbation in itself never made anybody incapable of sexual relations.

Sometimes it happens that a man does not outgrow his infantile relationship to his mother. He fails to mature emotionally, and can't arrive at an adult attitude to any woman. His attachment to his mother, though he doesn't realize it, is always in the way.

Once more: the aggressive side of his nature may have got dammed up. You see, in the male, aggression and sex are very closely bound up together. Biologically it is his role to pursue and possess the female. Some men, perhaps because they were so strictly repressed in childhood, can't assert themselves, and they can't summon up enough aggressiveness to take the initiative and play the man's part in the sex relationship. Perhaps it's worth while saying that most women like to find some male aggressiveness in their men. They want to discover an occasional touch of the cave-men; they want to feel themselves taken and possessed. If a husband seems terribly deficient in aggressiveness, a wife will very likely try all she knows to make him show that side of his nature. That's the explanation of a lot of nagging.

Now, a more frequent difficulty than failure to secure any erection is premature ejaculation, to which I have referred already. The semen is discharged either before union has been brought about, or so quickly afterwards that the wife has no chance to get satisfaction. Well, that's a pretty common happening in the very early days of married life, and it is nothing to worry about. But it is liable to cause an awful lot of trouble if the couple do not know that it is not unusual. The poor fellow is humiliated and disgusted with himself. If he has had fears about his sexual powers, as many men have, he says to himself, 'So I *am* going to be impotent after all!' He supposes his wife despises him—as possibly she does if she doesn't know that the mishap may occur and is not prepared for it. If it happens several times it may fasten a fear of failure on the newly married man. He thinks he is going to fail every time, and so is half-way to the very thing he dreads. He exercises all his will-power, but it doesn't do a scrap of good. He has a picture of himself failing, and there is a psychological law that, when will and imagination are in conflict, the imagination always wins. There is no reason, so far as I know, to suppose that *you* will have this difficulty at the beginning, but, if you should, don't let it worry either Jill or you. I remember a young husband who did run up against this snag writing to me, 'We laughed together over my failures—and now everything is all right.' How different it would have been if he had heaped reproaches on himself, and if his bride had made her feelings felt by blame or stony silence or tears! Premature ejaculation in these earliest days may be due to nothing more than nervousness, which is less likely to be troublesome if the situation, should it occur, is going to be met with the good humour and good sense of that young couple. Or it may happen because the newlyweds are inexperienced and a bit awkward, and don't find it easy to effect union just at first.

If the trouble doesn't quickly clear up of itself, don't let it drag on so that the fear of failure gets you down. Get advice about it. There may be some little physical trouble, as when the skin of the top of the penis is abnormally sensitive. There may be some psychological hold-up. Some men have quick ejaculation, for example, because they regard sex as nasty and their unconscious mind is saying, 'Get it over as quickly as possible and have done with it.' Sometimes there is no reason at all except that the couple don't have intercourse often enough, with the result that the accumulation of semen is so great that it discharges itself too quickly.

Sometimes the question is asked: How long *ought* an erection to last. There is no 'ought' about it in the sense that you can say a person's blood pressure or pulse rate 'ought' to be this or that. In point of fact, the time during which different men can hold an erection varies enormously, and so it does in the same man from one occasion to another. These figures, supplied by Dr Dickinson and Dr Beam on the basis of 362 cases, will give you some idea: Under five minutes, 40 per cent ('instantly', 12 per cent; two minutes, 4 per cent; three minutes, 24 per cent); five to ten minutes, 34 per cent; fifteen to twenty minutes, 17 per cent; half an hour or more, 9 per cent.

And, of course, women vary greatly in the length of time they require to reach orgasm. Fortunately, it generally happens that with experience of sexual life men are able to continue union longer, while women tend to reach orgasm more quickly.

Now, what makes a woman 'frigid'—i.e. incapable of experiencing sexual feeling?

It used to be said sometimes that certain women are born without the capacity for sexual satisfaction and that the characteristic is inherited. But it is now held that frigid women are not born but 'made'. It may happen because, as I was saying in a previous letter, they pick up from their mothers or other women the notion that sex is disgusting; because of shocks about menstruation or the processes of birth; because of an indecent assault or some other disagreeable sexual experience. Many women who would never have been frigid are made so at the very outset of marriage by the lack of consideration, coarseness, or even downright brutality of their husbands, who insist on their 'marital rights'. A lot of frigidity dates back to the wedding night, when a husband forced himself on a girl who perhaps knew little about the sexual side of marriage and was neither psychologically nor physically prepared to meet his demands.

Of course, not all women who fail to reach orgasm, even though their husbands are potent enough, are actually frigid. They are capable of a great deal of sexual excitement, but somehow can never quite reach the climax. That may be because they can't let themselves go with absolute abandon; they keep all their emotions, and not only their sex passions, on a tight rein. Possibly their inhibition is not strong enough to hold up all sexual response, but they have the feeling deep down inside that there's something wrong or indecent in just *giving way* to passion, which is necessary for complete orgasm. Fear of pregnancy, and in fact any anxiety touching the sex life, may also act as a brake. Orgasm may be held up by repressed hostility to the husband. The wife gets her own back by refusing him the gratification of giving her complete satisfaction, even though she is cutting off her own nose to spite her face.

Now, if Jill and you don't manage straight away to achieve mutual orgasm, what can you do about it? Let's set down the steps you can take:

(1) Treat it just at first as nothing unusual—and don't bother.

(2) If things don't come right quickly, see if your technique of love-making is satisfactory. Talk it over frankly, and get Jill to tell

you exactly what she feels is lacking. Try new positions and introduce variety into your love-making.

(3) Make sure there is nothing 'putting you off'. The utmost personal delicacy and cleanliness is necessary. Disgust will effectively put paid to sexual feeling, and any physical pain or discomfort may inhibit it.

(4) See that there is nothing in external conditions which is causing a hold-up; e.g., the fear of being overheard is sometimes a real snag in these days of housing difficulties.

(5) Go to a doctor and find out if there is anything physically wrong.

(6) If there is some psychological difficulty get competent advice about it. The illustrations I have given show how various and deep-seated the causes may be, and some of them call for expert help.

(7) Don't give up hope! Many couples have gone on for years hoping to achieve mutual orgasm—and at last it has come!

XIV

How often should intercourse take place?

In your last letter you ask me how often intercourse ought to take place. I don't think there's any *ought* about it. But, if we are going to use the word at all, I think all we can say is that it ought to take place as often as a couple of married lovers feel a mutual desire to express their love in that way, and can feel that it has been deepened and strengthened by that expression. I can't possibly tell you how often Jill and you (or any other couple) ought to have union. I fancy I can hear you murmuring. 'Thank you for nothing!' because I know that the question of frequency does get many young people guessing, and they want a sort of mathematical formula as an answer.

Well, if my reply is a right one, that isn't possible, because people vary as much in the strength of their sexual urges as in any other natural capacity. I have been hammering it in that in sex the physical and spiritual must not be separated, but to some extent the capacity of men and women for the physical expression of sex does depend on the actual make-up of their bodies. One person may be able to eat (and may actually need) quantities of food which would wreck the digestion of another in next to no time, and there is just as great a variation in sexual needs.

If you insist on mathematics I can't oblige you, except to tell you what various groups of people say as to the frequency with which they have intercourse.

Dr Dickinson and Dr Beam analysed the data given them by 526 couples, and they produced this table of frequency:—

    Daily or oftener, 16 per cent.

    Two or three times a week, 24 per cent.

    Once or twice a week, 20 per cent.

    Once in a week or ten days, 17 per cent.

    Once in a fortnight to a month, 10 per cent.

Once in two to six months, 2 per cent.

Once a year or less, 11 per cent.

Another authority, Dr Raymond Pearl, has shown that the average frequency varies with different age groups. Taking the cases of 257 men, whose average age when they married was 25, he found that intercourse occurred most frequently during the ten years from 35 to 45, and that sexual activity at 30 and 50 and at 25 and 55 were more or less comparable. He also found that within the age groups the frequency of intercourse varied with occupations and with the presence or absence of other satisfying emotional outlets.

I give you these figures only to show how people differ. For goodness' sake don't say, 'Jill and I are about 25 years old, so we ought to have intercourse x times a week.'

So much for mathematics! But I think I may be able to give you a few helpful suggestions.

First of all, never let your sex life degenerate into a routine. There are couples who make (or just drift into) the arrangement that they will have intercourse, say, once or twice a week. Sometimes they even have a fixed night, and, when it comes round, they have to go through with the business regardless of how they happen to be feeling, and even if one or both of them have no inclination at all. Each partner feels that, if the contract were not kept, the other would feel cheated and resentful. You see, couples who are so stupid as to let the whole thing become a matter of routine are not likely to be frank enough to say what their real feelings are. It sounds deadly—and it is!

I keep on coming back to the point that spontaneity is the secret of a happy sex life. Therefore it can't be regulated according to schedule. A couple who find that once a week is about their average may, for some reason, want intercourse two or three times within twenty-four hours, and then they may not feel the desire again for a fortnight.

I said in an earlier letter that too little sex love is probably a more frequent cause of trouble than too much, but I don't mean to imply that excess is impossible. Some men think that, whenever they awake with an erection, it is an indication that they have a sexual tension which needs relief. As a matter of fact, those erections generally have nothing to do with the state of their seminal reservoirs, but with the fullness of their bladders. Some men, too, have a false notion as to the value of their sexual powers. They think that ability to have intercourse repeatedly, whether their wives want it or not, stamps them as particularly fine fellows. They must really have a pretty poor opinion of themselves in other respects if they think that this is the one and only way of assuring themselves and their wives of their manliness and virility. Top of the list of causes leading to excess I should put common or garden boredom. It is literally true that people indulge in sexual intercourse because they don't know what else to do. Their lives are so dreadfully lacking in interests and in satisfying emotional experiences that they turn to sex for 'a bit of fun', and they are lucky if that does not soon begin to pall, seeing how little it must really mean to them. Their use of sex is a pathetic attempt to work off surplus emotional and physical energy. There is not much danger that a couple who have many interests in common, and who share a satisfying emotional life, will be tempted to sexual excess. Another cause of excess is over-indulgence in alcohol, which stimulates desire, and at the same time slackens self-control.

Of course, the frequency and intensity of desire is to some extent dependent on health. Fatigue lessens it. During the war some people turned to sexual adventures as a relief from strain, but many more, who were overworked and over-tired, found that they had little inclination even for the normal expressions of their love in marriage. Anxiety and worry have a depressing effect. It is a common experience that desire increases when a holiday relieves strain and fatigue. When fatigue diminishes passion, an understanding couple will not imagine that they are falling out of love with each other. It is foolish to try to whip up passion artificially. (Incidentally, don't have anything to do with the pills and things which are sold at certain shops at a high price as aphrodisiacs to increase desire. They are no good anyway—unless they work by suggestion!) And if only one of the partners is fatigued or below par, there is a sovereign opportunity for the other to show real love through patience and consideration. A husband who forces himself on a wife who is tired or unwell, or who makes life so unpleasant that she yields to him for the sake of peace and quietness, may find that he has implanted in her a permanent resentment and a dislike of the sexual life.

On the other hand, a temporary nervous fatigue or depression need not *necessarily* cause a couple to forgo physical union. The partner who is suffering from it is not very likely to take the initiative, but, if the other can arouse desire, the union may act as a release and a tonic, banishing weariness, soothing nerves and restoring the feeling of peace and well-being.

There is one possible difficulty which I must mention. I should think Jill and you are likely to be pretty equally matched in your sexual capacity, but, if marriage should reveal that one of you is much more strongly sexed than the other, you will need to handle the situation carefully and wisely. Some people have the idea that it is always the wife whose desire is less, but that is by no means the case. Unless the disparity is quite abnormal it will tend to adjust itself as time goes on, given patience and consideration in both partners, and provided that neither is held up by the sort of inhibitions I was talking about in an earlier letter. In the case of a wife, especially, the capacity for sexual desire and satisfaction is likely to increase if she does not receive too many setbacks and disappointments in the early days.

Well, I think it boils down to this: don't imagine that every stirring of sexual desire has to be gratified, or you may become bored with sex, just as a person who has over-eaten cannot stand the thought of food. Marriage isn't a sexual orgy, and there is a very great place for self-control; but, if you do not feel tired and on edge after intercourse, it isn't very likely that you are going to excess. And above all—avoid routine like the plague!

XV

The 'after-glow'

YOU may remember that I objected to the term 'sex act' because that suggests it begins when two lovers actually join their bodies—and I tried to show you that it *doesn't* begin then. In fact, you can't say when it begins. And by the same token, you can't say when it ends. Some time ago a young couple came to talk over their difficulties. Their problems were real enough, but I was immensely relieved (and a little surprised) to find that there seemed not to be much wrong with their sexual relationship. But I sensed there was *something* wrong, and at last I said to the girl, 'Come on—out with it!' 'Well', she blurted out, 'he *will* turn over and go to sleep as soon as it's over—and I don't want to'. I had to tell that young man that he was being really unkind—though I don't think he had the least inkling of it—and, further, that he didn't know what he was missing.

Many wives who never get orgasm, and are left strung up and unsatisfied, positively hate the man who gets *his* satisfaction all right, and then turns over and before you can say 'knife' begins to snore like a pig! But here was a girl who did get an orgasm, and then felt it was all spoiled because everything came to a sudden stop. It seemed to her like a very unfinished symphony. Luckily he was a husband who cared, and when I saw them next time all was well. (And no doubt the righting of that little matter, which had been a source of irritation to the girl all her married life, helped to smooth out the other difficulties.)

We saw that a woman is so made that her desire rises and reaches its climax more slowly than a man's. It also subsides more gradually. She doesn't, as a rule, want to break away from her lover and go to sleep as soon as the peak is passed. She still wants to lie in his arms, to caress him and be caressed while the tide of sexual feeling slowly subsides and calm and peace come over her.

It is a mistake if the husband suddenly withdraws, even if his wife has achieved a satisfying orgasm. He should remain in union with her while his erection gradually subsides, and that time, while they lie in each other's arms with a sense of having given everything, may be an experience of wonderful nearness. I think it was Van de Velde who first described this experience by a beautiful and expressive name—'the after-glow', and this is what he says about it:—

And the most profound and exquisite happiness which human beings can taste is tasted by couples who truly *love* one another, during this pause of respite and realization, after completed communion. Far, far more closely than even the rapture of mutual orgasm does this bliss and content of the *after-glow* unite true lovers, as they lie embraced, side by side, while nature recuperates, and their thoughts, in a waking dream, once more live through the joys they have experienced, and their souls meet and merge, even though their bodies are no longer linked. . . . The duration of the after-play cannot be suggested, because its end cannot be defined. In ideal marriage it passes imperceptibly into another prelude. For even after a lengthy interval, the memories and echoes of the last occasion live on, in a word of love, a look, a whispered reminder of shared delight and a tender hope of its renewal.

XVI

The why and how of birth control

So you've been having 'a terrific argument' with a friend on the question of birth control. Since you say 'he jumped on it with both feet' I suspect he was a Roman Catholic. The Catholic Church says officially that artificial birth control can *never* be justified—it is a 'sexual perversion' and 'a grievous sin'. An R.C. is bound to accept the ruling of his Church on these things, so, if your friend is a really staunch one, he couldn't very well do other than come down on the whole idea like a ton of bricks, whatever might be his own personal view (or his wife's) on the matter.

But, as you're not a Catholic, I take it you tried to approach the subject with an open mind, and to weigh up the pros and cons of it for yourself.

Well, the first question must be, 'Is it right?' If you answer 'Yes' to that, you'll have to go on to find the answer to a second question, 'What is the best method?'

Now, whether you believe birth control is right or not will depend pretty much on what you believe about the proper place and function of sex in married life. If you think that the *sole* purpose of our sexual powers is to enable us to have children, and that a couple should never have intercourse unless they deliberately mean a child to result from it, then the question is an easy one. I suppose there are still some people who take that view, but they must be very few. Not even the Catholic Church goes as far as that, for the one kind of birth control permitted is the restriction of intercourse to the so-called 'safe period'—in other words, the partners have relations for the sake of the satisfaction they get, and they *hope* they *won't* have a child. Of course, if you do go the whole way in holding that intercourse is *never* justified except for the purpose of procreation, the question as to whether birth control is right or not answers itself.

As you know by now, I believe that sex has a wider function in human life than the begetting of children. Among animals, I suppose, it has a purely biological significance. It is concerned with the reproduction of the species and nothing more. It is not a more or less constant urge having a direct or indirect influence on pretty nearly every aspect of life, and charged with emotional and spiritual as well as physical significance. The sex relationship, as I've said before, can be a tremendously strong bond between married lovers—a final expression of their love and intimacy bringing to the whole of their lives a balance and harmony. Therefore, a couple are justified in having sexual relations even if they know it is impossible for them ever to have children.

Now, one of the reasons urged against the practice of birth control is that it is so often abused. There's no getting away from that. It has led to a great deal of sexual laxity. People found that they could indulge their passions and for a few pence have just about 100 per cent certainty that they would escape the consequences. (Mind you, fear of consequences isn't much of a motive for doing what is right, but it worked sometimes. The true motive for avoiding laxity is an understanding of what sex really is, and an ideal of sex-love which lifts the whole thing on to a higher plane.) Even within marriage birth control can be misused. An official Catholic publication says: 'Those who limit their families artificially try to justify it. They say that they cannot afford children. They say that it is dangerous for the woman to bear children.' The sting is that people do make excuses of that sort to justify the use of birth control, when the truth is that they don't want children for selfish reasons. They want a car more than a baby, or they don't want their freedom to get out and about restricted, or something of that sort. But sometimes a couple *can't* afford children—or, at any rate, can't afford them as fast as they might come if the pair lived a normally satisfying sexual life. And sometimes it *is* dangerous for a woman to have children. So what?

Well, there are three things they can do.

They can just go ahead and chance what happens. But would you think that right if, for example, the doctor had told you flatly that Jill *must* not have any more children?

i

They can cut out sexual relations altogether. That is to say, they can in theory! A few couples with something like superhuman self-control or (more likely) sub-normal sexual impulses could do it in practice, for a time at least. But a normally sexed couple, in love with each other, couldn't do it for long without something going wrong. I said earlier on that I believe a couple, however madly they're in love, ought not to have intercourse before marriage. I believe they could and ought to keep themselves in hand to that extent. But it's another story altogether if they have lived together as man and wife, still love each other and want union. They may not be able to share a bed, nor a room, nor a house, for before long the tension may begin to get them down, and may show itself in all sorts of bothers and irritations, and finally perhaps in nervous breakdowns. I'm not saying, of course, that a couple can't abstain from intercourse for a reasonable time. I'm thinking of a situation which has to go on and on.

The third possibility, then, is to use a method of birth control. That can't be justified (let me say again!) if a couple for merely selfish reasons want to avoid the responsibility of parenthood. It is justified when (a) there are medical grounds for not having any more children or for delaying the arrival of the next one, (b) when there are good economic reasons for spacing out the arrival of the children, and (c) when there are *adequate* personal reasons of one sort or another. Obviously I can't mention every possible situation. You will have to decide for yourselves if and when you are justified in using birth control.

Now, suppose you do decide that there are periods in your married life when you are justified in preventing conception, what is the best method? I think you can apply three tests to any method: (1) Is it safe? (2) How far does it interfere with spontaneity? (3) Does it detract from the sexual satisfaction of either partner?

Reliability is obviously of prime importance—sometimes it may be a matter of life and death. In any case, unless the partners have confidence in the method they are using, they won't be able to abandon themselves completely to the enjoyment of their union. That underlying anxiety probably prevents a good many women from reaching complete satisfaction, and is perhaps the reason why some never do until they have passed the age when child-bearing is possible.

I must mention two 'methods' for the sake of saying bluntly that they won't do. One is what is called 'coitus interruptus'—which means that union is effected in the ordinary way, but the man withdraws his penis before ejaculation takes place. There's not a good word to be said for it; doctors and psychologists are agreed on that. Practised just occasionally, when both partners urgently desire union and no means of control is available, it may not do much harm, and it may be true that a small minority of people can make a habit of it and not be much the worse. But generally, if it becomes the regular régime, it plays up the nerves of both partners. The man gets relief of a physical tension, but very likely pays for it with a sense of frustration which makes him irritable or worse. The woman gets stimulated and receives no final relief. (It may happen, of course, that if the wife is quick to reach orgasm and the husband is slow, she may get to the climax before he has to with-draw, but that is certainly the exception.) And there is no after-glow. At the very moment when they want to be nearest to each other, they have to tear themselves apart. Moreover, this method hasn't a dog's chance of passing the reliability test. If the husband delays a moment too long he may be too late. And even if he gets clear in what seems to be good time he can't be sure. Before the actual ejaculation begins a microscopic sperm may have found its way out. (There are an astronomical number of them in each ejaculation, you will remember, and one is enough to bring about conception.) Even if a little semen touches the outside of the woman's organs, it is just possible she may become pregnant, for a sperm can find its way in under its own power. Apart from all the other objections, then, this method gets no marks for reliability.

Just about as unsatisfactory is the practice of restricting inter-course to the 'safe period'. In some popular books you are told when a woman's safe period is—but the books don't agree! I won't even tell you what they say, for, if ever you rely on the safe period and find it's not so safe after all, you shan't blame me! There are, in fact, some days between two menstrual periods when conception cannot happen, but just when that time is would have to be worked out in the case of any individual by scientific investigation—and even then there might be a mistake.

There's another objection, too. Most women, as you know, find that there are periods of a few days when they are apt to feel sex desire most strongly, and other periods when it is at a low ebb. Although, as I've said, nothing can be called a *safe* period, the times when conception is less likely to occur are, in many cases, precisely the times when desire is least easily aroused, so on all three tests this method gets a thoroughly bad mark.

Now, I could set out a long list of methods which employ some chemical or mechanical means to prevent conception, but there are really only two which are worth your consideration.

One is the wearing of a condom or sheath by the husband. If you get a good article from a reputable chemist, in theory it scores the top mark for reliability. But that's about all there is to be said for it. Many couples find that it wrecks spontaneity, for, unless the sheath is put on before love-making begins (which is impossible for some men), the love-play has to be interrupted by what is such a painfully artificial proceeding! Moreover many, both husbands and wives, find that it detracts from their satisfaction. Some husbands say that it hastens their reactions so much that their wives have no chance of satisfaction; others, on the contrary, find their sensations are so dulled that they can't reach orgasm themselves. Wives, too, often heartily dislike the contact with the sheath.

The most satisfactory method is the wearing by the wife of a rubber cap, which is fitted into the end of the vagina or over the neck of the womb in order to prevent the semen from entering the womb. This method has a high score for reliability if (but only if) the cap is properly fitted by a doctor or at a birth control clinic, and if all instructions given in connexion with the use of it are strictly observed. A woman who walks into a shop and buys a cap on the chance that it may fit is asking for trouble. This method does not interfere with spontaneity, since the cap can be put into place before the wife goes to bed—and it will be there if it is needed. And it does not detract from the satisfaction of either husband or wife, since neither can feel its presence.

Well, what are Jill and you going to do about it?

If Jill is in good trim and you can afford it, don't wait long before you have your first baby. And don't make too much of that word 'afford'. It doesn't mean waiting until you've got a car and a wireless set and every room furnished just as you would like. When you've got the essentials for your home with just a touch of beauty and comfort here and there, and a few pounds in the bank to cover emergencies, you can afford to start a family. It may be all right to have a few months just to get settled down together before the baby begins to come, but people who deliberately put it off for years sometimes find it difficult to readjust their lives to the new situation. They don't take kindly to the restriction of their liberty to get about together and do just what they like. Further, there's a lot to be said for beginning and completing the family while the parents are still young, and can share the fun and games with the children in a way they wouldn't be able to later on.

It is better—much better—if the first unions can be absolutely free from all interference with nature. But supposing you do decide, for adequate reasons, that you want to use some method of birth control, Jill should mention it when she goes for the pre-marriage overhaul I spoke about. She should get the doctor to fit her with a cap or arrange for it to be done elsewhere, if he feels, as some doctors do, that it is a specialist's job. It will mean that the hymen, if it is still unbroken, may have to be stretched, but there's no trouble about that, and, anyhow, as I said before, it is a good thing to have it done in order to make the first unions easier.

XVII

The importance of small things

How time flies! It doesn't seem a year since you wrote to me about your engagement, and here you are telling me all about the way Jill and you celebrated the anniversary of it. I am glad you have started the very sensible practice of remembering anniversaries. As time goes on, the number of days in the year which have some special significance for you will mount up and you won't be able to celebrate them all, but it is a good thing to call them to mind, and to mark a few of them by some little outing or gift to each other. I think most happily married couples have formed the habit of celebrating. It helps to keep something alive which is easily lost, and it is a good thing to have a few days in the year when our thoughts go back to what we were thinking and doing ten, twenty or thirty years ago. Sometimes, when we have lost our way a bit, it is useful to have some fixed point to which we can get back and start on the right road again. The anniversary of the wedding day can very well serve in that way, if we don't just let it slip by year after year unnoticed or with only a passing thought.

Some of the things that happy husbands and wives remember and speak about, when the days come round, would seem small and insignificant enough to outsiders. No doubt some of them *are* small, but our lives are mostly made up of small things. Oliver Wendell Holmes begins one of his books with the question: 'Is life a little bundle of great things or a great bundle of little things?' The answer to that isn't difficult. For most of us it is mainly a very great bundle of very little things.

You know, one of the secrets of life is to learn the importance of little things. In his autobiography George Arliss says that he was once making a film, and a certain scene had to be shot over and over again because a strange crackling noise was heard in the sound track. For a long time nobody could make head or tail of it.

Then they discovered that, when Arliss lit his pipe on the set, the particular tobacco he was smoking crackled, and the sound of it became tremendously exaggerated. What a detail to wreck a whole scene many times over!

It is true in all art that success depends on detail, as Michael Angelo said long ago. A great Russian painter one day corrected a pupil's drawing, so Tolstoy tells us. The pupil glanced at it and said in astonishment, 'Why, you only touched a tiny bit of it, but it is quite a different thing!' The artist replied, 'Art begins where the tiny bit begins.' As Tolstoy says, that is true, not simply of art, but of all life.

Believe me, it is true of married life. Most marriages which come to grief are not wrecked by big things, but by little ones—some of them as unregarded at first as the crackling of George Arliss's pipe. They may end up with some great wrong or unfaithfulness, and to people who haven't seen the inside the collapse sometimes seems very sudden. But it is not really so sudden as all that. The way for the final show-down has been prepared by the piling-up of little bits of selfishness, misunderstandings, irritations, jealousies and such things.

There is a great danger that, with the passing of the years, a husband and wife will come to take each other for granted. Then the little bits of courtesy and consideration which they delighted to offer to each other during the engagement will begin to drop out. 'Expect the romance of a home to end', says Dick Sheppard, 'when he fails to perform towards her those little acts of courtesy that he gladly offered her in the happy days of courtship, or she fails to acknowledge them with grace. It is good-bye to something essential, for instance, when he forgets or is too lazy to open the door for her, or she neglects to smile gratefully at him when he does.'

It is a thousand pities, too, when the little words of compliment and appreciation are no longer said. I have no doubt that you tell Jill a dozen times, whenever you see her, that she looks charming. (You do if you are an honest man!) And she likes to hear it even if she tells you not to be silly. But it will mean even more to her in twenty years' time, because she will find it harder to believe then than she does now, though it will still be true—at any rate, it will if you succeed in making her happy. We men are the worst offenders in not saying the little things which mean so much. Sometimes we grow so dull and stupid (or is it that we get so wrapped up in ourselves?) that we don't even see when our wives have a new dress on and are simply longing for us to notice it and say we like it. If they remain in love with us (and in spite of the cynics and the music-hall comedians quite a lot of them do) they want to look attractive for our sakes. Even if sometimes they derive a naughty pleasure from realizing that they look nicer than Mrs Jones over the way, our appreciation means a lot more to them than such a hollow triumph. So don't stop telling Jill you like the look of her when you've safely married her. And don't be so dumb as not to show your appreciation of little things she does in the house. After all, most women spend their days in the house, and it must be mighty dull sometimes. When a wife does something—whether it's a special culinary effort, the decorating of the spare bedroom, the arranging of some beautiful flowers, or the sewing on of a neat patch—and her husband looks right at it without noticing, it must be a bit dispiriting.

Some of us don't remember how much little gifts and surprises mean to a wife—especially the surprises. It is a good thing to celebrate the really special occasions, like the anniversary of the wedding day, by exchanging gifts, but perhaps the unexpected present, even if it is only a few flowers, means even more. After all, we may go on giving birthday and Christmas presents because it has become a habit, but the spontaneous gift which comes as a surprise shows that there was a real thought behind it.

Oh! and there's one thing more, but it's important. Don't forget to go on telling Jill, after you've married her, that you love her. Many of us men are not good at that. We can't see the need to be told our wives love us. We are quite prepared (in our colossal conceit?) to assume it. Whatever the reason, women—or most of them—either can't or won't take their husbands' love for granted. They want to be reassured of it. Especially as they get on towards middle life many wives fear that they are losing their attractiveness, and some even look with apprehension at the fresh young girls who seem to them potential rivals for their husbands' love. I am quite sure Jill will never have any need to fear that you will cease loving her. In her heart she will know you won't—but she'll probably need to be told it all the same. Women are like that—bless 'em!

D

XVIII

Squabbles

So Jill and you have been at loggerheads! I hope everything is straightened out by now. You don't say what the bone of contention was, but you give a hint of the situation—'We both had our own ideas about it, and neither of us would jolly well give way.'

I imagine this is the first time you have fallen out, so it is a good opportunity for us to take a look at the whole business of 'squabbles'.

There aren't many couples who get through the whole of their married life without an occasional upset, though it may not, of course, get to the point of a full-dress quarrel. I am sometimes told, 'We've never had a wry word in all the *x* years we've been married.' Honestly, I'm a bit sceptical when I hear that. Sometimes I can't avoid the suspicion that it's a mis-statement—to put it no stronger. I don't mean that the person who says it is necessarily lying. We tend to forget disagreeable things, and people who are very happy together may manage, without conscious self-deception, to forget the few times when things have gone wrong. And I don't deny there may be a few couples who achieved such perfect harmony from the start that they quite literally have never had a cross or impatient word. But as to the rest, I suspect that, if it is a fact that they have never had a wry word, one of them has made 'peace at any price' the prime rule of life, and has possibly been content to be a mere doormat.

Now, some marriages are a struggle from the very beginning. Each of the 'partners' is determined to come out on top, and they will fight until one gives in, until the marriage blows up, or until death calls 'Time' to the whole sorry contest. The two of them develop great skill in the use of their own particular weapons. Bullying and nagging are the most obvious ones, but there are plenty of others. A husband may become an adept at humiliating his wife in all sorts of subtle ways, especially in company. A wife may play the invalid, when there is nothing organically wrong with her, because thereby she hopes to force her husband to treat her gently and to wait on her, while at the same time she pays him out by putting him to a great deal of trouble and makes her 'illness' a silent accusation—'It was you who made me like this.' Tears, sarcasm, endless criticism, incitements to jealousy and all manner of things are in the armament of warring couples! As once upon a time in love, so now all is fair in war.

Often enough the reason for the struggle is that husband and wife feel inferior to each other, and each feels also the necessity of establishing superiority. One of the most delightful couples I have ever met were in that case. They had everything which ought to have made an ideally happy marriage, but endless irritations and squabbles were bringing them to the point of saying they couldn't go on together. Each felt contemptuous of certain things in the other. They were helped to understand that, in fact, each had unconsciously felt a humiliating inferiority to the other in some respects. So each was looking for things which would justify the feeling that the other was pretty poor stuff—and inevitably they were seing a lot that wasn't there. When they grasped the real situation and frankly admitted it to each other, their problem was solved. They could then admire the strong points in each other and accept—perhaps even help with—the weak ones.

Now, it would be easy to make out a pretty long list of things about which married people quarrel. It would certainly include sex, money, in-laws, the discipline of children and a good many other things which have been touched on in these letters. The plain fact is that if a couple want to quarrel they can always find a cause. I know you are just going to blurt out, 'That's silly. Who would ever *want* to quarrel?' Well, I have a notion that some people do like a good set-to now and again. You see, the heightening of emotion is generally pleasurable. That's why Juliet said, 'Parting is such sweet sorrow.' And some people would tell you that in a queer sort of way they got some pleasure out of air-raids during the last war. They were scared and thought them awful (as they certainly were), but there was a stimulus in the consciousness of danger, and so emotions of one sort and another were intensified beyond the pitch of ordinary life. Certainly emotions are heightened in a domestic row! Some people who are bored with the sameness of every day get a kick out of the excitement. And there's always the thrill of reconciliation, complete with tears and kisses. 'The falling out of lovers is the renewing of love.' So they say. But it's a dangerous game to play too often. One of the partners, at least, may get tired of it, and, longing for more settled peace, may find that the ardour of reconciliation begins to grow less. But, as I was saying, if a couple are given to squabbling, the slightest thing will afford a pretext, and before calm has been restored all the issues they have ever quarrelled about before, and half the things they said in those quarrels, will have been dragged up again.

There are no more irrational people on earth than lovers in the midst of a tiff, or a married couple letting themselves go in a domestic row. Most people don't argue very logically at the best of times, and one of the reasons is that emotions very easily twist thought out of the straight. Outside the realm of pure science, argument untouched by emotion is probably impossible—and not even all scientists can argue dispassionately about their subjects. Certainly not many people can argue about politics, religion, or sport, to say nothing of their personal problems, without the likelihood that emotion will sometimes get the better of reason. What hope is there when engaged or married people begin to argue? Before they have been at it ten minutes emotions will have torn reason to shreds, even in the case of the person who adopts the tactics of ostentatiously 'keeping cool'.

It is worth remembering that quite often a quarrel is a sign, not of a rift between the couple, but of something wrong elsewhere. Mr A. comes home morose and irritable, snapping at the children and complaining about everything. There is, in fact, nothing whatever to grouse about. His meal is as well cooked as usual, and the children are no more noisy. If Mrs A. ventures gently to point these things out, he immediately projects his bad temper on to her and accuses her of being in a vile humour. The children presently retire to bed in tears, and Mrs A. demands to know exactly what she has done wrong. She will then be met with a sulky silence or a stream of petty charges, without foundation, which will leave her bewildered. The truth is, of course, that she hasn't done anything. But it happens that he has had a particularly worrying day at the office, or somebody was promoted over his head, or the manager sent for him and gave him a good ticking-off. He would have liked to have gone straight to the boss and told him exactly what he thought of him for giving the job to that young upstart, while he (a much abler man, of course, and one who had given longer service to the firm) was passed over, and he would have given a lot to have told the manager a thing or two. All the way home in the train he has been thinking up what he ought to have said, and imagining the total annihilation of the boss or the manager. It would have relieved his feelings to say those things, but he didn't say them, so his feelings haven't been relieved! He must take it out of somebody or burst. He doesn't *decide* to make his wife and kids the victims; he's not such a cad as that. But as they happen to be handy and can't retaliate as the boss would have done, he unloads on them all the resentment and bad temper he has been bottling up. Or perhaps the shoe will be on the other foot. Mr A., after a harassing day, catches the train for home with a feeling of relief, and looking forward pleasantly to an evening of domestic peace. But for some reason, which he cannot guess, he finds Mrs A. in a highly explosive state, so that the most harmless word is likely to provide the spark. He doesn't know that she is simply working off on him her annoyance because a shopkeeper was abominably rude to her; her chagrin because Mrs B. has cut her; or the resentment she felt when she met Mrs C. all cock-a-hoop in a new rig-out, while she, who needed one much more, will have to make hers do for another year. The moral of it all is this: before you vent your spleen on Jill pull yourself up and ask whether she is the offender or whether your annoyance is really intended for somebody else. And, of course, that applies in turn to her.

Here's another tip. Be on your guard against tiredness. In an earlier letter I said that moods more easily get hold of us when we are tired, and we are certainly more apt to be quarrelsome. Perhaps you've noticed in driving a car that, when you get really fagged, your judgment isn't as sound as usual; you don't estimate distances so accurately, and you take risks that you wouldn't take at other times. And, when we're tired, our sense of perspective is apt to go haywire. We make big issues out of trifles, we say things we shouldn't dream of saying at other times, and our control of temper is precarious.

Now, suppose Jill and you have some point at issue between you which might lead to a quarrel if it weren't settled, what is the way to handle the situation? The answer is short: talk it out. Don't brood or sulk about it; get it into the open. Notice I said *talk*, not argue, it out. There's all the difference in the world. When a married couple begin to argue, they are both concerned to prove that they are in the right. They want to score points. But, when they settle down to talk it out, they are not trying to get the better of each other; they are out to help each other to get at the truth. They will not indulge in mutual recriminations and try to fix blame, but they will be ready to admit their own mistakes. A person who will never admit an error is impossible to live with! Such a fellow appears to be cocksure of himself, but the truth is he is so *unsure* of himself that he daren't admit he can ever be wrong. He argues unconsciously to himself: if I am wrong once, why shouldn't I be wrong all the time? And he feels that, if he confesses he has made a hash of something, he will give himself away and nobody will have any time for him. If a husband and wife are going to live together happily, they will have to gain such confidence in each other that they will not imagine the admission of a fault will make any difference to their mutual regard. Do you remember what I said about giving up poses?

When Jill and you settle down to talk something out, don't take up the attitude: I am a rational male. Women never can reason—they only jump to conclusions. Somebody has said that there isn't any difference between the sexes in that respect except that men, having jumped to conclusions, think up some reasons afterwards, whereas women don't take that trouble. And Jill, for her part, mustn't take her stand on 'intuition'. I think a great many women do rely on intuition more than men, and often it serves them very well; but it is good-bye to understanding when they set up intuition as infallible and flatly refuse to reason.

See to it that no sarcasm escapes you; that's fatal. And it is just as bad to say 'innocent' things in such a way that they mean something else. Do you know *The Screwtape Letters?* They are supposed to be written by one of the devil's chief agents to his nephew, who is just learning the art of tempting mortals. He says:—

In civilized life domestic hatred usually expresses itself by saying things which would appear quite harmless on paper (the *words* are not offensive), but in such a voice, or at such a moment, that they are not far short of a blow in the face. To keep this game up you and Glubose must see to it that each of these two fools has a sort of double standard. Your patient must demand that all his own utterances are to be taken at their face value and judged simply on the actual words, while at the same time judging all his mother's utterances with the fullest and most over-sensitive interpretation of the tone and the context and the suspected intention. She must be encouraged to do the same to him. Hence from every quarrel they can both go away convinced, or very nearly convinced, that they are quite innocent. You know the kind of things: 'I simply ask her what time dinner will be, and she flies into a temper.' Once this habit is well established you have the delightful situation of a human being saying things with the express purpose of offending and yet having a grievance when offence is taken.

Be sure that Jill knows just what you mean, and that you are clear about what she is trying to tell you. Not many people always express themselves with absolute clarity, and even the few who do are misunderstood occasionally because their hearers are apt to interpret their words in the light of the preconceived ideas which are already in their own minds. Many a man has gone about brooding for days over something his wife has said to him, and when at last it has come out, she has asked him in hurt astonishment, 'But how *did* you think I could have meant that?'

One of your greatest assets in these minor domestic crises will be your sense of humour. There's a lot of meaning in the phrase 'a saving sense of humour'. It can often save an awkward situation from developing into something serious. If a person is unfortunate enough not to have a sense of humour, I don't know what is to be done about it; but if you have one it can be developed like any other quality. Of course, nobody ever yet admitted he hadn't got a sense of humour. I suppose you would need a sense of humour to see you hadn't got one! But the truth is that some folk are without it. Often the reason is that they are too self-centred. The fellow who is absorbed in himself can never really laugh. He may go through the motions and emit a noise, but there is no mirth in it. But even the person who can see jokes may not be able to laugh at himself when he looks ridiculous. Perhaps he is not sufficiently grown up. Children can never laugh at themselves, but we have to learn to do it as we leave childhood behind. You see, we should never be pompous or stand on our dignity if we had learned to turn the spotlight of humour on ourselves. And we should never get into a temper over trifles—or for that matter over anything—because a person in a temper is an absurd and laughable sight. If we could see a sound film of ourselves going off the deep end over nothing, it would probably cure us for good and all! They are a happy couple who both have a lively sense of humour, for many a spot of bother will dissolve in laughter. It will enable them to keep their sense of proportion, and that is all-important in married life, which is mostly made up of little things The vast majority of domestic squabbles arise out of some trifle which has got magnified, so that, for the moment, it absorbs all the field of vision and blots out everything else.

There's just one more point. Never sleep on a squabble. 'Let not the sun go down upon your wrath' is sound psychology. If you happen to have let the sun go down, don't let the bedside light go out upon it anyway. If you are in the middle of a quarrel, there will probably be a good deal of lying awake and tossing about while you both think bitter thoughts, and conjure up in your minds the stinging retorts you might have made. And don't forget that, when you do eventually fall asleep, your unconscious mind will still go on working. The angry, ugly thoughts will go down into the deeper levels of the mind and do their nefarious work there. You and Jill had better make a solemn vow that you will never go to sleep with a squabble on your hands, and that you will never let yourselves get into the impasse where both of you want to make it up and neither of you will pocket pride and take the first step.

Well, there you are. Talk out your bothers with honesty and good humour. Never go to sleep with one on your chest, and when you have settled it up write *finis* under it—*and never hark back to it again!*

XIX

Managing the family finances

IT may sound unromantic and all that, but I am going to talk in a most matter-of-fact way about money. You have heard the ridiculous misquotation. 'Money is the root of all evil.' That's nonsense. Money—like sex—is neither good nor bad in itself; everything depends on the use you make of it. The quotation, of course, should read, 'The *love* of money is the root of all evil.' That's sense, for if it isn't the root of *all* evil it is certainly the source of a great part of it. The love of money has made a hash of plenty of marriages, and I am not thinking only of the gold-diggers who marry for the sake of it. Not that many people love or want money for what it is in itself. I suppose nobody does but the true miser, and he is a rare bird. People want it for what it can buy—power, prestige, a passport into the upper levels of society, luxury and so on. I should say that the blundering mismanagement of money has spoiled more marriages than the love of it. When one listens to the stories of marriages that have gone awry, it comes up again and again with monotonous regularity. I don't say it is always a prime cause of disagreement, though it sometimes is, but it turns up everlastingly as an important side-issue or aggravation.

So I advise Jill and you to go carefully into every side of the £ s. d. question, to safeguard yourselves against all the snags, and to think out a thoroughly sound working arrangement. Perhaps you are saying, 'That would be a waste of time. When two people love and trust each other as completely as Jill and I do, there's no need to treat marriage as a business proposition and have safeguards to see we don't do each other down. All that can be left to look after itself.' Let's get this straight. I keep on referring to marriage as a partnership, and the analogy is not a bad one here. When two people go into partnership they enter into a contract, as the law puts it, *uberrimae fidei*, i.e., requiring the utmost good faith. If a partner in a firm is untrustworthy, suspicious, jealous and selfish, the finest deed ever drawn up will not suffice to maintain harmony. And the best thought-out scheme, covering every aspect of domestic finances, won't keep a marriage from going to pieces if even one of the partners becomes untrustworthy or any of the other things I mentioned above. On the other hand, the existence of a soundly drawn partnership deed has often been instrumental in preventing the growth, among members of a firm, of grievances and disputes which have plagued the life of another firm whose deed has been hastily and thoughtlessly thrown together. You see, the 'utmost good faith', even when it undoubtedly exists, may not be enough in itself. And that is certainly as true in marriage as in business life. I have known couples, who undoubtedly loved and trusted each other, between whom grievances still arose, just because they had not thought out their financial problems and had not seen the implications of them.

Now, it seems to me that the first thing Jill and you will have to do is to get some idea as to what your standard of life is going to be. And you will do well to pass a strong and unanimous resolution that at the start, and all the way through, it is going to be a way of life which you can afford. So many young couples begin wrongly by trying from the outset to live above their incomes. They want to live in a house they can't afford, and buy furniture they can't afford, and have a car they can't afford, and entertain on a scale they can't afford, and—well, there's no end to it. This business of 'trying to keep up with the Joneses' is madness. We can't afford to have a baby *and* a car—so it will have to be a car! So we will inflict on ourselves a real deprivation and do violence to the best and most altruistic side of our nature in order that we may enjoy a few more superficial pleasures, and cut some sort of a figure in the set we want to mix with! Mind you, I am not suggesting that a couple should marry before they can see their way to set up even a modest home and keep it going. That would be sheer irresponsibility. It doesn't make for a happy and harmonious home life if there is the knowledge, always hanging like a cloud over everything, that, do what you will, you can't make ends meet, and if, every time you sit down in the armchair, you wonder whether it will be there tomorrow, or whether the furniture people will have fetched it away because the instalments are miles in arrear. It is a terrible pity when a young couple, who could live happily and without anxiety in a modest way if only they would be content with it, land themselves in endless trouble and bickerings because they must go and overshoot the mark. A married woman, who has handled these things very well and is now getting on in years, said to me recently, 'It seems to me that a lot of young people nowadays want to begin where we are leaving off'—and I think there's a lot in it.

Well, having agreed on the cardinal principle that you will always live in a way which you can properly afford, the next step is to put all your cards on the table. If your marriage is going to be a real partnership, it must be so in financial matters as in all else. So you mustn't have any secrets from each other. Perhaps you'll hardly believe it, but a great many men never tell their wives what they are earning, and would make no end of a row about it if they were asked. There's a Gilbertian situation for you! One half of the 'partnership' is not allowed to know what the available resources are, and therefore can't possibly judge whether a share-out (if there is one) is fair or not. It's a hangover from the times when men regarded women as their chattels, and kept them absolutely in their power by holding on tight to the purse strings. Unless you want to go back to the Dark Ages, tell Jill exactly what you've got and what you are earning and make that your practice all the way through. And, of course, that goes for her, too. I don't know whether she is going to keep on with her job for a bit. There isn't much to be said against it so long as the thing is kept in proper perspective, but Jill must realize that she is asking for trouble if she puts her job first and her home nowhere, and she will make a big mistake if she keeps on putting off the arrival of your first baby so that she can hold on to her job a little longer. I'm not going to discuss the vexed question as to whether married women should have careers or not. I have known it to work out very successfully, but those women did solve the problem of keeping home and job in proper perspective, and were, perhaps, particularly fortunate in some respects. Of course, if it becomes certain that there isn't ever going to be a baby and adoption is ruled out, there's something to be said for a wife's having a career of her own. Anyway, I hope you won't object to Jill having a job on the absurd ground that it is a blow to a man's pride if his wife works, because it looks as though he can't 'keep' her. Dr Johnson got hot about the collar over that point—but that was in the eighteenth century!

I'm getting badly side-tracked! I was saying that if Jill earns anything, whether it's more or less than you do, it all goes, with your salary and the interest on any savings or legacies either of you may happen to have, into the common pool. Then you can sit down together as equals with one vote each—no matter who has put most into the pool—to plan how your resources are going to be used. Yes, *plan*, for you must have a system, even if it isn't a very elaborate one. I'm not going to suggest any rigid system. There are so many ways in which married couples arrange their money affairs quite successfully that to say this is *the* way to do it would be absurd.

Obviously, any system will involve a bit of elementary book-keeping, for there must be some record of income and expenditure. It doesn't matter in the least whether it is the husband or the wife who keeps the book. It looks like a job for the one who has the better business head, or who is the more methodical, because it won't do to keep accounts by fits and starts. Accounts kept with reasonable accuracy will enable you to check up from time to time so that you can see where the money is going. If you find after a while that it is difficult to make ends meet, and you have not kept any accounts, you will be in an awkward corner, because you will have to cut down somewhere, and you won't know where it can be done. Whereas, if you have kept track of your outgoings, you will be able to sit down together with your book, total up the amount of money spent on various things and say, 'Well, we can't cut down on this, but we've spent more than we can afford on that.'

When you have reckoned up the total amount coming into your home you ought to make one or two deductions straight away.

First, you must take off what must be paid in taxation; though nowadays P.A.Y.E. will very likely do it for you, neatly if not painlessly!

Then you should decide on a fixed proportion to be given away to objects and causes outside your home—to your Church or various kinds of social work or whatever you may happen to be interested in and think worth supporting. I know some people would loudly protest against making this sort of benevolence a first charge on income. Well, if they think that it's a good thing to spend every penny on themselves or if they think that just the odd copper (if they happen to have one to spare) is enough for 'charity', there's not much to be done about it. I'll only say that if they imagine they'll find happiness by spending everything on themselves and their own pleasures, they're barking up the wrong tree. Self-centred people don't get within sight of real happiness. Even if it's not much you can afford to give away, set aside what you can before you begin to work out what you have to spend on yourselves.

Next decide on a fixed amount of saving. This, again, might be a percentage, though the percentage should be stiffened as the total income rises. In the earlier years the main, if not the only, form of saving should be life assurance on the life of the earner. And probably the best kind of policy is the endowment policy, timed to fall in just about at the probable age of retirement. That is better than the whole-life policy falling in at death, though the premium is naturally a little higher.

Now, what about your book? An accountant friend of mine, who has reduced the keeping of domestic accounts to a fine art, gives me the following list of headings, which, he says, are wide enough to cover most circumstances:—

1. Rent, rates, insurance (not including National Health or life), and house repairs.
2. Repairs and renewals of furniture and equipment.
3. Heating and lighting.
4. Housekeeping (food, laundry and cleaning materials only).
5. Payments for domestic help (if any).
6. Personal expenditure of (a) husband, (b) wife.
7. Postages, stationery and telephone.
8. Fares (and car expenses, if any).
9. Medical and dental expenses.
10. Presents.
11. Expenses *re* children: (a) clothing;
                             (b) education;
                             (c) sundries.

12. Entertainments and miscellaneous expenditure.
13. Holidays.
14. Charities.
15. Savings (including life insurance premiums).

Well, there's the whole thing set out for those who want to make a thorough job of it. But my friend mercifully concedes that this classification may be too elaborate for the average couple, and that it can be considerably compressed so long as the main outlines are not blurred (e.g. Nos. 1, 2 and 3 might be combined). The keystone to the whole thing is, he says, No. 6, with the distinction kept between (a) and (b). In that he is certainly dead right. How many heart-burnings (and worse) would be saved if all couples had that heading in their domestic accounts—even if they did not have any other!

What often happens is this. The man spends what he likes on his own 'needs'—as defined by himself, of course! He gives his wife a sum for housekeeping. Sometimes it is a settled amount—again often settled by him—sometimes he hands out more or less as he feels inclined. And No. 6 (b) never enters into his calculations. In other words, his wife hasn't a penny that she can call her own. If she wants a little money for even the most pressing personal needs, she must do one of two things: (1) Ask her husband for it with a feeling of humiliation—and perhaps be met either with a refusal or an open or veiled accusation of extravagance. (2) Try to get it out of her (perhaps all-too-meagre) housekeeping allowance. If she is driven to get it from this source she will very likely have a guilty feeling every time, as though she were appropriating trust funds!

Well, that sort of situation is intolerable for any self-respecting wife, and ought to be just as unbearable for any self-respecting husband. Remembering that all they have belongs jointly to them both, they should agree as to the amount which each can spend *without any questions being asked*. If neither knows how much the other is spending on personal needs or amusements, how can either judge whether his or her own expenditure is reasonable? Where one does not know, one tends to suspect; and that way danger lies. Couples may differ as to the proportionate amounts which husband and wife ought to have. In theory 50-50 seems fair, but many men will be ready to agree with their wives (!) that a woman's needs are more costly, especially as regards clothing. My accountant friend plumps for 50-50, but adds, 'If the husband feels he is getting the better of the bargain, he can, with good judgment, redress the balance at Christmas or when a birthday comes, by giving handsomely. I once knew a husband who, alone and unaided, would buy a hat as a present for his wife and bear it home in triumph. I reject this particular way of redressing the balance with some emphasis! One further point as regards a man's presents to his wife. There may be occasions when 'something useful for the house' is really appreciated, and, if it be a labour-saving device, can be defended. It can be overdone, however!'

Talking of presents, No. 10 is meant to include all presents which are given jointly, whether to friends or relatives. As a general principle it is wise to keep the cost pretty level as regards relatives on each side of the family. Presents to personal friends of the husband and wife ought perhaps to come out of their respective personal allowance; if that is to be the rule it must be taken into account when the budget is being made up.

And now I suppose you are saying, 'All very nice, no doubt, but does the crazy fellow think we shall ever remember to make a note of everything we spend? We shall forget more than half.' Well, that's up to you. I don't imagine that you will get every single half-penny down. I did hear of somebody who tried keeping domestic accounts, and who had a column headed 'G.O.K.', which always contained the largest expenditure. She explained that it meant 'Goodness Only Knows'! The difficulty is, of course, to get down all the little oddments—the fares, the newspapers, the cigarettes and so on. However, you probably won't be terribly far out if you make a habit of jotting down your casual expenditure at the end of every day. That can be acquired, like any other habit, with a bit of persistence, and you will probably soon become so interested in seeing how the money goes that it will cease to be an affliction. Anyway, whether it is good fun to you or a weariness of the flesh, you will be wise to keep accounts, during the early years, at any rate, if you want your marriage to be on a sound financial basis. If you think the keeping of reasonably accurate accounts is really quite beyond you, you had better use a number of little boxes or something to hold the money allotted under the various headings, so that the limit on *personal* expenditure is kept to.

It is worth while to take the trouble to think and plan so that you may avoid the little rubs which, believe me, have been known to take the bloom off marriages which promised as well as yours.

XX

More about the family finances

YOUR battery of questions was not altogether unexpected. Let's take them in order.

You say Jill is anxious to know just what is to be included in 'Housekeeping'. Well, nothing but the three items put down under that heading—food, laundry and cleaning materials. Everything else (like domestic help if you're lucky enough to have any!) is provided for under some other heading. You ought to give Jill an amount to cover those three things and see to it that she does not have to meet all sorts of other expenses out of that fund. She will then know exactly what she has to manage on. If sometimes she has a surplus don't expect her to hand it back to you. Let her build up a sort of reserve fund to cover extra expenses when, for example visitors come. And if there should be a real rise in the cost of living and she quite reasonably asks for an increase, don't begin blowing her up for extravagance!

What about running up bills ? Well, you'll need to keep a watchful eye on that. You obviously can't keep accounts if it is all one to you whether bills are going to be paid this year or next, or at any rate you'll always have to be calculating your outstanding liabilities and allowing for them every time you want to see how matters stand. It's a hopeless way of going on if you don't settle up bills either at once or at regular intervals, and, moreover, it isn't fair to the tradesmen who allow you credit. It may be a good arrangement for Jill to pay a good many of the bills, which aren't properly in her department, when she is about town on her shopping expeditions, but in that case she must be regularly reimbursed or her own financial arrangements will break down.

Yes, I think it is a good thing for a wife to have her own banking account. In Victorian times the running of an account was thought to be quite beyond the intelligence of women. They were quite content to leave such mysteries to the almost supernatural wisdom of their husbands. Most of them probably had no choice anyhow!

You have raised some very interesting questions about a wife's position with regard to property.

It is certainly wise to keep a list of any items of furniture which the wife brings with her, inherits or acquires in any other way than by means of money provided by the husband. There are circumstances of financial disaster in which this information may protect her position.

From the point of view of the State marriage is, of course, a contract, but it has features which distinguish it from all other contracts, and perhaps that is why the law has lagged behind modern thought in its readiness to recognize the change in outlook which has occurred and is still going on. Generations to come may find it impossible to understand why the twentieth century was almost in sight before the right of a married woman to the separate ownership of property was established. You can sometimes read in the newspapers reports of cases in which a marriage has broken down, and the husband is challenging his wife's right to hold on to money or investments which she has put aside during the marriage. Those cases stir up a good deal of discussion and correspondence in the papers, and show how much people's outlooks on these things differ. Of course, the law ought to be so framed that justice is done to a wife if her marriage breaks up (and even if it doesn't), and perhaps there are more changes to come. But we are not concerned with the law at the moment, nor with what ought to be done when a couple get across each other so badly that they refuse to go on living together. We want to know what is a fair arrangement, when things are going well, in order that misunderstandings and estrangements may be avoided.

Now, what about property (money, investments, houses, or what you will) which one party owns before marriage ? Not so long ago that problem would have been solved by the husband as easily as rolling off a log. Unless he were prevented from doing so by involved legal processes, he would automatically have appropriated whatever his wife possessed on the principle that 'what's yours is mine and what's mine is my own'—and nobody would have thought any the worse of him for that. A more modern attitude is to regard both the capital and the income from it as belonging to the recipient absolutely. Those who want to make their marriage a complete partnership might go a good deal farther and forthwith divide **any** windfall which comes to either of them into halves, so that the income from it goes equally to both. Probably that way of doing it would be a bit too idealistic for most ordinary mortals, and perhaps it is a case for a compromise. So what about this? Let any capital which either possessed before marriage continue to belong to the holder, and let any legacies or gifts which happen to come along after marriage be retained by the one who receives them, but let the income from all the lot go into the common pool, so that it is shared equally by both parties. That seems a fair working arrangement, and if the marriage did end in disaster it would have certain advantages, for, without any arrangement being necessary, each partner would have:—

1. Anything possessed as investments before marriage.
2. Anything coming by legacy or otherwise since marriage.
3. One-half of anything saved during the period of the marriage out of the joint income of the two parties.

What about money invested out of income earned after marriage? Generally only the husband will be earning. Is he, then, to invest anything left over and reckon it his own property? On the principle of partnership any surplus should be set aside in equal portions in the separate names of husband and wife. This is one point at which 'the utmost good faith' comes in, for the arrangement involves implicit trust that neither party will, at some time or other, realize on the investment and use it for personal purposes. And interest would naturally go back into the common pool.

One last bit of advice—and this is certainly sound, however much you may want to argue about what has gone before! Endless trouble is caused, especially to women whose husbands die, because people do not take the simple and obvious step of making a will. It is most important that you, at any rate, should do it at the time you marry. Don't say it's hardly worth while because you haven't got much to leave, or that you feel very well and have no intention of dying for some time to come, so there's no hurry. How do you know you won't walk in front of a bus or become a target for some marauding germ? If you have any consideration for Jill, you'll make your will. Or, more correctly, you'll *get it made*. Don't buy one of those ready-made forms from a stationer's and think you can do it just as well yourself. Even a simple will needs to be drawn up properly. So go to a solicitor. He won't charge much, and it will be worth the money to know that you haven't left tangles to be unravelled when you are out of the way. And Jill and you should discuss with him how you want your wills framed so as to provide as far as possible for the children who may come along later. This is important, especially if both of you should die before the children are grown up and launched into the world.

Well, whenever you think or talk about finances, get that word 'partnership' firmly into your heads. It's pretty shocking when a husband, because he brings home the money, thinks he can say how it is to be spent without consulting his wife at all; and it is only a little better when he thinks he always has the casting vote or the right of veto. And I confess I am sorry for the husband whose wife has money 'of her own', and who is not allowed to forget it. A wife, who dominates or humiliates her husband because she happens to 'have the money', ought to be kicked. Of course, if the wretched man married simply for her money he's only getting what he asked for. All the same, if the wife allowed herself to be married for money she is just as big a fool, so she may as well keep quiet. It is another story if the man married the woman because he really loved her, and would have been just as keen to marry her if she had been as poor as a church mouse. If the wife ever makes him conscious that it is *her* money which enables them to do this and that, she is not worthy of his love and is false to the ideal of partnership. And if the husband ever makes his wife feel dependent on him because he happens to bring home the wherewithal (while she perhaps works far harder at home!) he is so far from understanding the meaning of marriage that he had better have remained a bachelor!

XXI

Hire-purchase

I AM interested to know that Jill and you have been discussing the pros and cons of hire-purchase. A lot of young people are in your street—they want to set up a nice, well-equipped home, but they haven't a lot of ready cash on which to do it. Hire-purchase seems to offer a solution of their problem, and *up to a point* I think it does. (You're quite wrong, you see, in supposing that I wouldn't touch it with a barge-pole!) But I think you need to understand just what hire-purchase is and to be very sure about what you're doing.

It is possible to buy a house and pretty well everything in it on the instalment system. Yes, even a house, if you buy it by means of a building society mortgage, as many young people do. You make regular payments, which represent interest on the sum outstanding plus something in reduction of the purchase price or the sum borrowed. Now, that's the essence of hire-purchase, and there can be nothing wrong or improvident about buying a house in that way. In fact, when their elders hear that a couple are doing it they nod their heads approvingly and say, 'What wise and thrifty young people!' But there are snags about hire-purchase, which don't appear in the transaction of buying a good house through a reputable building society. So we had better look into it a bit more.

It is important to realize, first, that *however the terms may be set out*, you have to pay in due course the price of the goods plus something for the privilege of not paying the whole amount on the nail. This extra amount is really interest, and the rate per cent may vary enormously. A building society, for example, charges a fairly modest rate—at the moment it is generally about six per cent. On things like motor-cars and television sets it is generally in the region of ten per cent.

Now, of course, the attractive advertisements (complete with picture of the newlyweds rapturously choosing their furniture under the benevolent eye of the salesman, who appears to be saying 'Don't mention it' to any suggestion of payment!) and the agreement which you have to sign does not mention 'interest'—which might put you off. Often the existence of interest lies hidden in the fact that the price charged for goods sold under this system is higher than would be the case if the goods were being bought for cash down. The basis of the transaction is that it gives the purchaser the immediate satisfaction of a need (though it's a bit of a stretch to call it a *need* sometimes!) which would otherwise have to remain unsatisfied until enough money had been saved to pay cash on the spot. The danger of hire-purchase is that it presents a standing temptation to people who want to get hold of everything that takes their fancy without asking whether they can afford it, and without all the tiresome delay of saving up for it. It's so fatally easy. After all, the amount of an instalment doesn't sound much if you say it quickly! But if you let yourself go in an orgy of hire-purchase, you are likely to find yourself in a mess later on. This way of buying things is only justified if two conditions are fulfilled:—

(1) You must be clear that, under reasonable conditions of wear and tear, the article will have been paid for in full long before it is worn out or obsolete. To have payments spread out over, say, four years for an article which can't be expected to last longer than five is running things far too close. A couple I know bought a vacuum cleaner by instalments soon after they were married. They were a bit doubtful about the wisdom of it, but it was the only way of getting one. It turned out to be a godsend, and, as it was a good one, it is still going strong years and years afterwards.

(2) There should be a pretty real assurance that you have a margin of savings which will be ample to cover the repayments as they fall due. It won't be much comfort to you, if you borrow through a building society, to calculate that the repayments amount to only £20 a year more than you would have to pay in rent for the same house, if your annual savings are likely to fall short of £20 a year. In the same way, if you are thinking about the furniture you are going to put into the house, it would be absurd to acquire all the stuff you want on a contract involving you in payments of £50 per annum if you know that you will be able to save

only £25 a year towards it. The law protects the hire-purchaser from rapacious suppliers, who used to impose unreasonably harsh penalties on those who failed to keep up their payments; but the law can't encourage people who enter in a scatter-brained sort of way into contracts which they ought to have known they had no hope of carrying out.

Well, then, go easy with the hire-purchase system if you use it at all. *Don't* use it except for something which is an essential or very near to it. And an essential isn't something which tickles your fancy or which you think it would be nice to have. Don't get tangled up in instalments for luxuries or things which will wear out almost as fast as you pay for them. Be satisfied in your own mind that, if you buy anything in this way, you would be able to sell it at any time for at least as much as you still have to pay, and that it is something you will still be using long after the happy day when it really has become your own property.

XXII

Houses and furniture

FINDING or building a house and turning it into a home is a couple's first experience of practical joint planning, and it's such good fun because they both have to use their imagination in terms of 'we' instead of 'I'.

If you are likely to live in the same town for a good long time, there is everything to be said for owning your house. I don't suppose you will be able to put down all the cash for it outright, but, as I said in my last letter, this is certainly a case in which the instalment plan is justified, for, if you get a decent house, it won't be tumbling to bits before you have finished paying for it. A good building society—and there are plenty of them—will help you here.

If you are going to buy a house which is already built, make sure that it is one worth having. There are others! Between the wars jerry-builders had a glorious time opening up new building estates and putting up houses as quickly as they could be thrown together. Those gentlemen know a thing or two. They can make a house attractive with a few gadgets and a cheap touch here and there, but the less said about the workmanship and materials the better. There are many points which need to be considered in buying a house, and the amateur who thinks he knows all about the business is asking for trouble and generally gets it. The only sensible way to go about it is to have the house vetted professionally by an architect or surveyor, who will see that the drains and damp-proof courses are all right, that there is no dry-rot about the place, and so on. His fee will be money well spent.

I don't know what sort of a house appeals to Jill and you. People are apt to say of architecture, as of music or pictures, 'I don't know much about it, but I know what I like!' The implication is that everything is just a matter of taste, and that there are no real standards of what is good and bad—which seems to me plain nonsense. There are good designs—and there are bad! You should hear an architect friend of mine on what he calls 'ye olde worlde half-timbered horror' beloved of the jerry-builders. 'Extravagant, overhanging gables and meaningless excrescences', he says, 'cover up bad proportions and sell the house into the bargain.' In the Middle Ages a site was cleared of trees and they were available as framing to be filled in with wattle and daub or something which happened to be handy, but to try to recapture the picturesque effect by sticking creosoted boards on the face of brickwork is nonsense. ('Dishonest', my friend calls it. As you see, he happens to have a conscience.)

I shouldn't wonder if Jill and you have a dream house. Why not build it? It will be fun planning it out together. When you have your ideas in shape, you will have to call in an architect and ask him to prepare plans for you. He may say some of the things you want can't be done, but if he is the sort of man who has some imagination and tries to get inside your minds, he will probably produce something better than you first thought of. Moreover, as he will recommend a reliable builder and will keep an eye on the construction, you will know that you are getting good value for your money. See to it that Jill has a fair say, that she gets at any rate most of the cupboards she has set her heart on, and that the height of the kitchen sink is such that she won't either have to stand on tiptoe or get chronic backache through stooping.

Well, suppose the house is up. Next it has to be decorated. Here the aim ought to be simplicity. The room should be a background for the furniture, and distempered or plainly papered walls make a better setting than heavily patterned paper with the inevitable floral frieze.

Colour can be introduced in the furnishings, but they should not all be gay, or it will not be possible to see the wood for the trees. A brightly coloured cushion, lampshade, bedspread or curtain can be the highlight in a balanced scheme of things. There is plenty of scope here for individual taste. Indeed, the decoration and furnishing of a house ought to be the expression of the individuality of the people who live in it. I have stayed now and again in the houses of wealthy people, who have called in a firm of furnishers and said, 'Now fit up the place—expense doesn't matter.' The result may be artistic (though sometimes it doesn't look so to me!) but it doesn't in the least express the personality of anyone in the house. Anybody else might just as well live there. My architect friend says that in the course of his work he often goes into houses which have been furnished by well-known firms, and he can generally tell at a glance which of them has done the job. You are not likely, I imagine, in the early days to be in a position to call in furnishers and say, 'Here's my cheque-book— just carry on', but, even if you are, don't do it. Don't ever do it! Let your home be your own creation.

When you have got together what you must have at the start, the best and certainly the most interesting way is to add to your furniture as you come across things which appeal to you. It is good fun to hunt for them on holiday, for example. That way of making your home brings more satisfaction than fitting it up from top to bottom with suites and things chosen from a catalogue or a warehouse.

Wherever and however you buy your furniture, remember the importance of quality. Articles may look attractive when they are brand new, but the point is, how will they look in ten or fifteen years' time, when they will, perhaps, have had pretty rough usage from a vigorous and growing family? I don't agree with young-sters being allowed to spoil or wreck perfectly good furniture if they've a mind to. (Some people seem to think their children will suffer from repressions if they are not positively encouraged to smash up the happy home!) But furniture is bound to be put to a pretty severe test when there are children about the place. Good quality things will survive the ordeal, but cheap stuff will be turned into shabby wreckage. Apart from the greater satisfaction of having good articles around you, it is obviously sound economy in the long run to put quality before quantity.

I don't know how you feel about antiques. That, again, is a matter of taste. Personally, I would prefer them any day to the ultra-modern stuff—chairs made of bent tubing and so on. There's nothing to be said for cluttering up your home with things just because they are old. (What are museums for?) They must be beautiful or useful or both, as many old things are. If you buy antiques, you are not likely to know whether you are getting genuine articles or not. Experts often enough can't tell a really good fake from an original. But a fake, i.e., a piece of furniture made after an old model from old wood, may be a beautiful thing and worth having. It usually is, for otherwise the maker wouldn't think it worth while to spend so much time and skill on it. The difference between a good fake and an original is academic and need concern only the expert. There is, of course, a distinction between the fake and the 'repro', which is made from new wood and is much cheaper. The makers of reproduction furniture say, in effect, 'You won't be able to get an original and you may not be able to afford a fake, so why not have something as nearly like it as you can get?' The 'repro' manufacturers even go so far as to exaggerate the features of the prototype by shading the 'worn' parts, and thereby only succeed in gilding the lily.

In recent years new furniture has become available, which is well made, practical and good to look at. The Scandinavians have developed the trend much more than we have, but we have been influenced by them and are producing very good designs which can be recognized by their utility, comfort and simplicity. The furniture is generally made of light-coloured wood— probably a reaction to the tendency to splash dark stain about which has prevailed for so long. Cheerful fabrics and upholstery are used to set off the simplicity of the natural wood. You can see examples of this kind of craftsmanship in exhibitions and in illustrated periodicals.

Well, put as much beauty as you can into your home. You don't need a lot of money for that. You can go into houses where everything shouts at you about money, but there is not a bit of good taste or beauty or homeliness to be seen. And you can go into others where money has never been plentiful, but a couple have waited and saved and gathered about themselves things which are a joy to them, pictures which they do not grow tired of looking at, and books which have become friends.

Oh, there's one snag which crops up occasionally. Bride or bridegroom wants to import loads of things from the 'old home'. He or she has grown up with them, and they are cherished because all sorts of associations cluster about them. But they mean nothing to the other partner. No reasonable husband or wife would object to finding a place for a few of the other's household goods. But I'm thinking of the *un*reasonable person who wants to fill up the whole place with what has been begged, borrowed or inherited, so that the other partner can never feel, 'This is *our* home. We created it together, and, even if there's nothing very magnificent about it, it does express our personalities.'

XXIII

Friendships and jealousy

I HAVE been very interested to notice how often you mention your friends in those newsy letters, which tell me all about what you are doing, and I am so glad you often speak about '*our* friends', by which you mean friends whom you and Jill have in common. That's a grand thing, which is just one more augury for the success of your married life.

You see, the real wealth of our lives depends so much on our friendships. As wise old Aristotle put it, 'Without friends no one would care to live, even though he had all other goods except them.' Without friends life is a poor thing. In fact, it isn't life; it's only existence. And friendships can make all the difference to married life.

I'm so glad, then, that you talk about '*our* friends', because it is not by any means always like that with husbands and wives. Sometimes each has a separate set of friends. The man has his own circle of cronies whom he goes off to meet at his club or 'the local', and his wife may have her old school friends or some others. Sometimes the husband (I am afraid it generally *is* the husband) is rather ashamed of his cronies, wouldn't like his wife to meet them, and would never dream of taking them home. Now, a home into which people do not come as the friends of husband and wife, and equally welcomed by both, is a poor sort of place. Make your home hospitable, so that your real friends will like to drop in. And let them take you as you are. No doubt there will be Occasions when you will want to get out all the nice china and things you had as wedding presents, and entertain in style. But your real friends— the special ones—won't want to feel they're always visitors being fêted; they'll want to feel that they *belong*.

It sometimes happens that a couple, who had friends enough in their single days, rather shut themselves away when they get married. It isn't that they mean to be unfriendly, but they get absorbed in each other and their new home. They don't *want* anybody else—for the time being, that is. They are always saying, 'We really must ask Bill and Mary round—haven't set eyes on them since our wedding.' But somehow it doesn't come off, and soon their friends begin to think they have been pretty badly dropped. Then, when the newlyweds, finding that their seclusion is beginning to pall a bit, want to take up the friendships again, they are quite pained by the coolness with which they are received.

Sometimes it is only one of the pair who is responsible for the lack of friends. He or she is a bad mixer, likes 'my home to myself and can't stand troops of people about the place.' That is pretty tough on the other partner if that one happens to be a friendly and expansive soul. The unsociable half of the partnership ought to make every effort to get to like company. The reason for withdrawing into a shell may be away back in childhood. As a child he (if it is 'he') may have been subjected to an overdose of the 'little-boys-should-be-seen-and-not-heard' stuff; or he was weakly or handicapped and could not join in games, so that he felt an outsider, or he was not allowed by a fussy or snobbish mother to play with the other children round about, and so on. It may be only a case of taking the plunge, with the sympathetic encouragement of his wife, and he will discover he is not such a social failure as he thought. Anyway, if he can't break out of his shell, he ought not to deny his wife the joy of friendship. If he can't endure anybody about the house, he should encourage her to have her friends in when he can conveniently arrange to be out, and he shouldn't object if she sometimes leaves him to his own devices while she has an evening out with them.

The bugbear in some homes is jealousy. Sometimes a husband or wife violently objects to the other having any friends at all. That may arise from sheer selfishness—'You ought to give all your time and attention to ME!' Sometimes it is due rather to a lack of self-confidence. The one partner somewhere deep down inside feels inadequate and is afraid that, if the other finds outside companionship stimulating, he or she will no longer be wanted or will, at best, have to take second place.

Now, the mention of jealousy brings us up against the most difficult part of this question of friendships. What about friendships with the other sex? On this matter there are two extreme attitudes.

Your very 'modern' person will say: 'Why, of course there must be friendships with the other sex—plenty of them! How far should they go? Just as far as you like—all the way if the urge is there. Jealousy? Now, really, my dear, do remember we're not Victorians! *We* agreed before we were married that we'd each have a good time in our own way—and no questions asked. What? You don't think we can love each other very much? Stuff and nonsense! Of course we do!'

But do they?

And here, at the other end of the line, is a husband or wife who is tortured by jealousy. She (for convenience we'll keep to that pronoun, though it may as likely be 'he') won't let her partner out of her sight. She is in a turmoil if he is in the company of an attractive woman—or even one not so attractive! She can see looks pass and signs of understanding where none exist. She imagines 'situations' and suspects cunning plots to deceive her. The poor fellow is bewildered by her recriminations, and, do what he will, he can't dispel her jealousy. If he bears her reproaches in silence or makes a mild reply she says, 'There, you see, you can't deny it!' If he grows indignant, she retorts, 'If there was nothing in it you wouldn't fly into a temper!' So what?

Well, there is a pathological element in that unreasonable sort of jealousy. Sometimes it arises from a deep feeling of inferiority. The wife is all the time asking (perhaps unconsciously), 'What chance have I against all these more clever and attractive women?' (They may not be more clever or attractive except in her imagination.) Sometimes she is repressing a desire to be unfaithful herself, and she has a sense of guilt about it which causes her to imagine and condemn in her husband what she would, if she could only admit it, like to do herself. (Let me say again that all this may be equally true of a man.)

Now, is there some more reasonable position between these two extremes? This morbid jealousy has made hell of a good many marriages, but, on the other hand, if *nothing* can excite jealousy, is there any love between the couple? You can find your own answer to that one!

But one thing is clear to me. No husband or wife should do anything to give the other reasonable cause for jealousy. And men ought to be particularly careful, knowing that the male is by nature a polygamous animal. On the other hand, a wife who has no reason to complain of her husband's fickleness ought not to be perturbed if he looks longer than is strictly necessary at a pretty girl!

And I hope we can agree on two more points.

Neither husband nor wife should have friendships with the opposite sex which need in the slightest degree to be concealed from the other partner. If everything can't be open and above board, there's something wrong.

And neither should have intimate 'platonic' friendships. Sometimes a person who says a friendship is 'platonic' is talking humbug—and knows it. Sometimes it may be said sincerely enough, but who knows that a friendship between two normally sexed people will always remain so? Certainly *they* don't.

Friendships with members of the other sex are enriching, for women have much to give to men and men to women, and husbands and wives must have a mighty idea of their own adequacy if they think that no other man or woman can give anything which they cannot.

Obviously the ideal situation exists when husband and wife have men and women friends who belong to both, so that they share these friendships like everything else.

Well, go ahead and make your friendships. And see that you keep them in repair. They will enrich your life now, and perhaps still more as you get older.

XXIV

'In-laws'

WHILE we are on the subject of relationships with people outside the home, I think I ought to say something about 'in-laws'. Some people, reading that sentence, would say grimly, 'The trouble about my in-laws is that they are too much *inside* our home—a lot too much!' Dean Inge said once that many could sing fervently (but in a sense the writer didn't mean!) a line from a well-known hymn, 'Peace, perfect peace, with loved ones far away.' Jokes against mothers-in-law are still part of the stock-in-trade of comedians. A foreigner who listened to broadcast variety for a year might be forgiven for thinking that his wife and his mother-in-law are the two chief pests the average Britisher has to contend with. (Perhaps these are more or less universal forms of 'humour'— I don't know.) The fact is that relationships with in-laws are often a source of very great happiness. They present no problem of any kind and are an enrichment of life for everybody concerned. I happened this very day to read a passage in Mr Jack Jones' *Me and Mine*, in which he was talking about his wife's relationships with the members of his family: 'My parents and brothers and sisters', he says, 'were as much hers as mine'.

All the same, it is no good blinking the fact that in-laws can provide some thorny problems and be the cause of as much bitterness as almost anything in married life. And, while I think the comedians are unjust to mothers-in-law as a whole, I suspect that they are most frequently the cause of the trouble, while Dad, more or less ineffectively, does his best with the oil-can.

As we shall see, the fault is not always on the side of the in-laws, but there are some parents who commit deadly sins against the happiness of the young people.

There is, for example, the parent who won't let go. In a previous letter, you may remember, I wrote about the blight of possessiveness. Sometimes a mother tries to bind her son to her (especially if he is an only son) with bonds that he will never be able to break. She begins to clamp them on him even while he is a baby. She tries to make him dependent on her so that he will never be able to do without her. She won't let him learn to do things which he ought to do for himself lest he should break away. She poses as the utterly devoted mother, and probably really believes she is. In fact, she in making a bid for his undivided love and devotion because she needs it for her own emotional satisfaction. She is really seeking something which she has failed to get from her husband and her marriage. She will never be able to surrender the boy to another woman. She will very likely try all she knows to prevent him from marrying at all, and, if she is defeated in that battle, she will still fight on. She will still try to hold first place in his affection, and may even go all out in subtle ways to drive a wedge between him and his wife. She will be continually in his home, if she has the chance, and will complain bitterly if she is not always received with open arms by her daughter-in-law, who, of course, regards her as a dangerous rival. If her son is not always on her doorstep (preferably unaccompanied by his wife, for that allows more scope) she will reproach him for his neglect, saying, in words or looks, 'And after all I've done for you!' If only she could see into the depths of his heart she might be appalled to find a terrible hatred and resentment, and a desire to break free from her. But she has done her work well. The bonds, forged through the years, are strong. He may not be able to admit his hostility even to himself, so he defends his mother against the natural and justified resentment of his wife. He won't hear a word against mother! It's pretty tough on the girl, who sees her marriage being undermined, and feels she is up against forces she can't contend with.

Then there's the parent who *will* interfere. She is not so terribly possessive, but she thinks that nobody can possibly look after her child properly except herself. She is continually in a flat spin because she thinks her son's or daughter's health isn't what it was. 'I'm sure your house is damp.' Or 'I don't believe your shirts are properly aired. That's why you get all these colds. Now, when you were at home I always . . .' And a lot more in the same strain!

Naturally it gets a thousand times worse when the first baby arrives. 'What can that slip of a girl know about bringing up children? And all these modern ideas she gets out of books or somewhere! Won't have the baby picked up when he cries! Well, I shall pick him up when *I'm* in the house, and she can like it or lump it.' Sequel: a heated scene in which wife tells husband that she hasn't been able to get on with her work all day because baby has been crying and wouldn't stop. 'He was all right until *your mother* came to stay. I'm not going to have her interfering in future. I'll bring up my baby in my own way, and if she doesn't like it she can keep clear.'

Again, there's the parent who thinks that the prospective son- or daughter-in-law is not good enough. Sometimes the judgment happens to be right. The 'old people' weren't born yesterday, they have seen a good deal of life, and may have a pretty shrewd idea of what goes to the making of a happy marriage. They wouldn't say the same about every girl, but they can see that the one Tom has chosen just isn't the girl for him. But Tom is blindly in love, won't be put off, and is all the more determined to go ahead. A good many unhappy marriages might have been prevented if young people had listened to their parents—when they happened to be the right sort of parents. But I'm thinking of parents who would blackball any girl young Tom happened to be keen on. That might be because, seen through their rose-coloured spectacles, Tom is such a perfect example of all manly virtues that the feminine paragon who is fit to be his partner is not to be found anywhere. Or their objections may have nothing to do with character. It may be a matter of money or social position. Some parents are consumed with ambitions for their children. You see, their children are a sort of extension of their own egos, and they are seeking a vicarious compensation for their own frustrations and failures in what they hope will be the brilliant careers of their children, so that a match which gives a fillip to their expectations is the only one which can satisfy them. All the qualities which make a good husband or wife go for nothing if the forthcoming marriage does not obviously advance worldly prospects.

I must watch my step here, or I may give the impression that I think all the troubles are due to the stupidity or selfishness of parents—and that is a long way from the truth.

Just as there are some parents who won't let go of their children, so there are some children who won't grow into independence of their parents. They may set up a home of their own and earn their own living, but emotionally they are still tied to their parents. Nobody in that state can really leave father and mother and cleave to a wife. Of course, a man can be a devoted son and a devoted husband at the same time, but trouble comes if he can't outgrow his infantile attitude to his mother, so that with him it always remains mother first and wife nowhere.

Many people can make the necessary emotional adjustments when they are shown where the trouble lies, but there are obstinate cases of 'fixation' in which emotional development has been almost completely arrested. The man or woman is unconscious that the infantile attitude to a parent still exists and blocks the growth of normal feelings for the partner in marriage. In some cases the help of a psychologist is needed before the roots of the trouble can be brought up into consciousness and dealt with.

And what about the silly trick of idealizing parents and holding them up as an example ? Is a wife likely to be kindly disposed to her mother-in-law if she is constantly being told that as a cook she isn't in the same street ? Or will a husband who is next door to helpless with tools like his father-in-law any better for frequent reminders that 'Father is such a handy man about the house' I am sure that many people do carry in their minds a much over-painted picture of the parent of the opposite sex with which they openly compare their partners, and are surprised at the resentment they arouse and the sarcasm of the retorts they provoke.

Sometimes, I suspect, a young wife has a feeling of inferiority to her mother-in-law. Perhaps the girl has had a business or professional training, and doesn't know a lot about running a house. Mother-in-law is so frighteningly efficient in everything, and a son who has lived for years in such a perfectly organized home will be bound to notice the difference and (so the poor girl supposes) reflect daily and hourly on her incompetence. Her pride is hurt. She dislikes her mother-in-law, perhaps deliberately neglects her home so as not to challenge comparison, and makes disparaging remarks about women who can't think of anything beyond housekeeping. The implications are not likely to be missed, and the challenge will be taken up by a loyal son.

Sometimes difficulties arise because husband and wife come from families with different traditions or social standing. The wealthier or more cultured family may, of course, adopt a snobbish attitude. On the other hand, they may be far above that kind of thing, but the man or girl introduced into the family from a rather different way of life may come with such a sense of inferiority that it will be easy to imagine snobbery where none exists. It may be that the family which feels itself socially inferior will say that the intruder who has been introduced into their circle gives himself airs. In such cases husbands and wives will need thick skins if they are to avoid complications with in-laws, and a good deal of patience while mistaken notions are being proved false.

Well, that leads us to a few general principles which may be useful in a difficult situation.

It is always worth while making an effort to understand an in-law's point of view. A young wife might find her resentment abating a little if she tried her utmost to appreciate the strength and tenacity of a mother's love (even if she knows there is a selfish element in it), and if she could realize how difficult it can be for a mother to resign to another woman's care a son over whom she has clucked and fussed for twenty-five or thirty years. It would be worth while to put up with a good deal rather than to counter an attempt to drive a wedge between husband and wife (damnable though it is) by trying to drive another wedge between mother and son. And when that son is regarded as the epitome of all virtues, of whom no woman can ever by worthy, a wife who knows the shortcomings that a doting mother will never see, can find scope for a sense of humour which may literally be 'saving'.

Next, husband and wife must realize that their first loyalty is to each other. Without that loyalty the situation is desperate. If necessary, both must give their respective families to understand quite clearly that they are not prepared to listen to criticism of the other partner. And if, for example, his mother is bent on interference and will not let his wife be mistress in her own house, a husband must say kindly, but with all needed firmness, that he cannot allow that state of things to go on. It may not be easy to take such a stand, and his mother, until she accepts the new situation, may be mortally hurt, but he may have to choose between that and a grave injustice to his wife, coupled with the possibility of wrecking his marriage.

Neither husband nor wife must seek allies among their own people if a domestic difference should arise. Many a squabble which would never have amounted to very much if the couple had kept it to themselves, or had sought impartial advice, has become a war to the death because one (or both) of the parties has called on the clan to rally round and see justice (?) done. I don't mean that they must never go to a wise parent, brother or sister for advice; it all depends on whether the relative really is wise and is capable of taking an objective view of the situation. Often what is sought is not advice and help to solve the problem, but sympathy and support in carrying on the struggle. And some parents are only too willing to take up arms without regard to the rights and wrongs of the matter. There are foolish women ready enough to welcome a daughter who runs 'home to mother' after the sort of tiff that most couples would take in their stride, instead of telling her to go back and sort out her difficulties with her husband in a sensible way.

It all comes to this: both partners must do their best to make friends of their respective in-laws. Difficulties and prejudices must be overcome by persistent goodwill and refusal to take offence—which doesn't mean making a doormat of yourself. That sounds like a counsel of perfection, for many people find that nobody causes their hackles to rise so quickly as their in-laws. But it will often work in the end. Perhaps that young wife who resents her mother-in-law's competence and feels she is always being criticized would find the whole atmosphere changed if only she could bring herself to *ask* the help and advice of the older woman. And if all the goodwill and patience in the world fails to achieve anything, and the in-laws really prove 'impossible', let the partners remember that they married each other—and not each other's families!

Avoiding some common snags

I N these letters I am concerned only with getting Jill and you well
and truly launched into married life, and I am not going to be
drawn into a discussion of all the questions about bringing up
children which you will have to face later on. But I think I ought to
say something about the coming of the *first* child, especially in so
far as it affects your relationship with each other.

Many women go through the months of pregnancy with next to
no trouble, and say, when it's all over, that they hardly knew they
were having a baby. A few unlucky ones have a bad time all the
way through, and a lot have bad patches, but for the most part keep
pretty fit. When things are not going too well, a great deal can be
done to lessen the difficulties by the understanding and co-
operation of both partners, and the husband can be of real help
both in his sympathetic attitude and in all sorts of practical ways.
And he jolly well ought to be, for in this matter, at any rate, his
wife is certainly carrying the heavy end of the stick.

Of course, her own mental attitude to the situation will make a
lot of difference. It used to be believed that the thoughts and
experiences of the mother during pregnancy would have a great
effect on the character and even on the physical features of the
child. There was an old superstition that if a mother saw a hare, the
child would be born with a hare-lip. I once heard a doctor say that
some women seemed to think that if they caught sight of a man
with a peg for a leg, the baby would be born with a wooden leg
complete with a brass ferrule! Modern science says that the mental
and physical make-up of a child is determined by the combination
of genes it receives from its parents. A mother can't ensure that she
will produce a handsome boy by spending hours in a museum
looking at carvings of Greek athletes, nor can she endow him with
a genius for music by attending concerts! That doesn't mean

that a mother's mental attitude has *no* effect on her baby. Her state of mind will certainly influence her own health, and that will have something to do with determining whether her baby will be strong and contented or weakly and peevish. Resentment and anxiety certainly don't help.

Well, a husband ought to understand if his wife is sometimes a bit anxious (after all, she is taking some risks), or if she is occasionally peevish because she is feeling out of sorts. He must realize, too, that during pregnancy women sometimes develop strange and unaccountable likes and dislikes, and he must show himself as accommodating as possible, though that doesn't mean that a pregnant woman can consider she has a prescriptive right to have every foible, however unreasonable, instantly gratified. The more rational her way of life, the happier the months of pregnancy are likely to be.

The essential point is that the husband should try, even before the baby arrives, to make his wife feel that he is in partnership with her in this as in all other aspects of their life. He can't bear the pain for her, but he can do a great deal by sympathy and help to alleviate it, and he can show her that the responsibilities and burdens of parenthood are going to be equally shared. If that is his angle, he will be able to help by taking an interest in all the mysterious preparations for the coming of the baby, in the getting together of the necessary things, and so on. (I've heard it suggested by the way, that some young couples, in their natural desire to have everything 'nice', are apt to prepare rather too lavishly, and to waste on unnecessary things money which they would be glad of later on.) And the husband, who has really entered into the situation will be able to give his wife a hand over any bad patches by helping her to think of the happiness in store when the immediate discomforts and difficulties are over and forgotten—as they very soon can be.

There's one question you may want to ask just here—what about intercourse during pregnancy? Ought you to cut it out? Medical opinion is pretty well unanimous now that in moderation it does no harm up to, say, six weeks before the baby is due. Just occasionally a woman finds the idea distasteful, but generally sexual desire is not decreased. In many cases it actually becomes much stronger, partly perhaps because the fear of pregnancy, which is so often in the back of a woman's mind damping down her sexual ardour, obviously doesn't operate. Many doctors say it is wise to avoid the few days around the time when the monthly period would have occurred, because there is more chance of a miscarriage just about then. Of course, the husband must be careful and not too energetic in his movements, and, especially as time goes on, he must see that his weight does not press upon his wife's body. That can easily be got over by choosing a suitable position. If pregnancy is not absolutely normal, you should ask your doctor whether it is safe to have intercourse, and you should also get him to tell you when you can resume it after the baby has been born. Some husbands, I am afraid, are terribly inconsiderate, and force themselves on their wives without regard either to their health or feelings, with the result that they cause lasting resentment. On the other hand, a woman should realize that a long period of abstinence imposes a considerable strain on most husbands who love their wives, and they ought to do all they reasonably can to relieve the tension.

Well, now, let's assume that the young Jack or Jill has duly arrived. The coming of the first baby is something of an emotional crisis in the lives of most young parents. Quite properly, of course, they are fairly bursting with pride—but it ought to be pride in each other. You have perhaps met the new father pushing the pram and puffing out his chest, and by his very demeanour calling out to all the world, 'Meet my son! Alone I did it!' The cheek of the man! This supreme bit of creative work, which they have achieved together, ought to give a young husband and wife a new significance in each other's eyes and should forge a new and unbreakable bond between them. Often it has a very bracing and healthy effect. It leads them to give their lives a general overhaul because they do want, for the sake of their child, to make a good job of living. It gives them a new sense of purpose and direction. In short, it causes them to take themselves more seriously, which is a good thing, if they don't take themselves *too* seriously.

But the situation calls for an even deeper emotional adjustment. Hitherto husband and wife have held undisputed first place in each other's affections. That goes without saying if the marriage has been a real one. But what about this young 'interloper'? How is he going to be fitted into the picture? What sometimes happens is that he completely usurps his father's place. The young mother seems to have got all she wants and to have achieved self-fulfilment. Her husband then becomes almost unnecessary to her except as a convenient provider of the means to keep the home going. She gets completely absorbed in her baby, has no time for her husband, and perhaps loses all desire for the sexual expression of love. The husband is made to feel an outsider, grows resentful against his wife and against the child, and perhaps seeks consolation among his male cronies or in the arms of another woman who 'understands'.

On the other hand, the husband may be to blame for a difficult situation. Especially if he is himself of the spoiled-child type, he may resent the fact that his wife no longer gives to him her undivided attention. Some little things which used to be done for him don't get done now. Of course they don't, for the simple reason that his wife just hasn't time, and not because she loves him less. But he sulks or complains.

Both these attitudes are silly and unnecessary. A wife, who lets her husband be crowded out, is stupid and unkind, but a husband, who resents sharing her love and care with another life which belongs to them both, is equally blind and unreasonable. The one satisfactory way to solve the problem is to realize that there is no question of priority in affection. The child must be taken up into the love which each has for the other. The mother will not love her husband less because a new love has entered her life; indeed, it will be an extension of the love which she has always had for her husband. As for the child, he must be helped to feel that the love of his parents *includes* him. It is a dreadful thing if he feels that one parent resents him; that he has ousted one from the other's love; or that both are competing for his affection and preference. He should feel sure that his mother and father love each other, and they should not be afraid to let him see they do, though they must remember that to make love to each other in his presence, so as to make him jealous, is unpardonable. They should show him that they love him, too—that all three are enfolded in one great love. And they should not be afraid to express their love for him. What some psychologists have called the 'taboo on tenderness' can have a devastating effect on a child. How often a man or a woman who has been dogged all through life by a sense of insecurity will say, 'Oh, yes, I expect my parents loved me, but they never *showed* it!' Well, then, the child must be made to feel that in the love his parents had for each other there was a place already prepared for him. Then he will fit naturally and happily into the home.

Let's go back for a moment to the idea of partnership. You will have to make that a very practical matter, putting it as much on the 50-50 basis as the nature of the case allows. There are men who seem to think that the children (however many there are!) are the wife's job. Father goes off in the morning as the bread-winner, and when he comes home in the evening he doesn't expect to be bothered with troubles about the children. When they get past the baby stage he may like to play with them for a time before they go to bed—but that must be the limit of his commitments. I wonder how often I have heard wives complain that father comes home in the evening and finds in the children a relaxation and relief from the bothers of the office. He hasn't had them on his hands all day. They haven't driven *him* nearly to distraction. So they regard him as a jolly and tolerant playfellow who lets them do as they like and is so much better-tempered than mother! Yes, he may (as he says) have had a wearying day at the office, and it *is* a good thing that he should play with the children, but he ought to try to enter into all the cares and irritations of the family life, and not just skim the cream off it.

You had better begin to do all sorts of things right away, so that you get your hand in. And, at the first possible moment, get Jill to give you a lesson in bathing the baby. Of course, you'll think you are going to drop the slippery little rascal or that he'll break to pieces in your hands, but he'll survive—and so will you! And learn the gentle art of putting on napkins. You'll be no end proud of yourself when you are proficient! Take your turn in getting up at night if he's not well and somebody has to go to him. And as there will be more chores to do and Jill will have less time to do them you will be able to make yourself useful in that direction. One good thing which came out of the last war was that many men who had regarded household chores as 'woman's work' found that they are often arduous, that they require a very varied skill, that they can be dreadfully monotonous, but that withal they can be good fun when two people go about them in a team spirit.

There's just one other point. You must find some satisfactory solution of the problem of outings. Just think of the situation which often arises. All through the courtship and the first months or years of marriage a couple have been free to go about together as they like. Then comes the first baby, and somebody has to be tied to the house every evening. Now, a couple who aren't prepared to make some sacrifice of freedom for the sake of their child ought never to have had one. (I don't think they ought even to have married, but we'll let that pass.) But here's the rub: so often it is the wife who makes *all* the sacrifices. The husband gets out and about; she is cooped up night after night in the house. He keeps up all his interests; she drops all hers. Is it surprising if she becomes resentful? Obviously, if it is a real partnership, the husband will sometimes stay in and they will have the evening at home; that will be no hardship if they have cultivated interests together. Sometimes he will stay in so that his wife can go out and keep up some of the outside interests which prevent a woman going stale. Then, when it is his turn to go out alone, she won't feel that she has had a raw deal. But they must also arrange sometimes to get out *together*—even if they can't manage it very often. That's a real tonic, or (if I may mix the metaphors) a wonderful lubricant which helps the wheels of marriage to turn smoothly. You must solve this little problem somehow. If you happen to have parents or relatives living near you, it may be solved for you. If you are not so lucky, look round for somebody who will sit in occasionally while you go out. A good many people who live in digs or institutions, where there is not much privacy, are glad of a quiet evening by a homely fireside. Even if you have to pay somebody now and then, it will be a good investment. I have heard of a few young people who 'solve' the problem by just locking the kids in and going off. That's shocking. The danger of fire and so on may be pretty remote, but there is a very good chance that one evening the youngster may awake from a terrifying dream, call his parents, and find that he is in the house *alone* with his terrors. That is enough to destroy his sense of security and leave its mark on him

all through life, and it isn't very likely that he will ever really trust
the parents who have let him down so badly. By the same token
don't ever deceive him by pretending that you are not going out.
Be quite open about it, and let him see the person who is going to
keep house. If you accustom him to this from his earliest days, he'll
take it quite as a matter of course and won't mind in the least. I've
no patience with mothers who say, 'Oh, I couldn't do it! I'd never
leave my child with anybody!' That's bad for a mother, for it
easily leads to a sense of superior virtue or even martyrdom. And
it's bad for the child. It doesn't help him to achieve independence
if he is not allowed to feel himself safe unless mother's watchful eye
is on him. Of course, no responsible parent would leave a child in
the care of just *anybody*, but there are sensible and reliable people
who are quite capable of seeing that a child—even yours or mine!
—comes to no harm for an hour or two.

Well, think out these little problems together so that, when
young Jack or Jill arrives, you will have a feeling of fulfilment
unspoiled by any sense that your life together has been cramped
or narrowed.

XXVI

The wedding

TAKE it gently, my lad! You've got caught up in the maelstrom of wedding preparations, and, like nearly every man who has gone before you, you're half-dazed and inclined to grumble that you don't know what all the fuss is about. You can take it from me that no mere man ever does properly understand the why and the wherefore of these things! I have no doubt you would, as you say, like to carry Jill off to that little country church you discovered on your holidays, when you were feeling so close to each other, and there get married all by your own two selves. It is such a personal thing between the two of you that you can't see where anybody else comes into it, and you 'simply can't stand the thought of gaping crowds'.

Well, don't be too hard even on the gaping crowds. You'll probably have to run the gauntlet of them before you manage, with Jill on your arm, to sink exhausted into your taxi! I admit I can never quite understand the crowds, large and small, who gather outside churches and register offices, quite ready to wait half an hour for the thrill of seeing two total strangers emerge as man and wife. No doubt the cynic, who believes the unsuspecting bridegroom is walking to something worse than a lingering death, would liken them to the crowd who hang about outside a prison on the morning of an execution—

> 'Waiting, as empty people always wait,
> For the strong toxic of another's hell.'

I daresay the crowd, hoping to catch a glimpse of the newlyweds, waits with mixed motives. Some of them have a pornographic interest; some like to imagine themselves in the shoes of the 'happy couple' and think how they would love to start all over again and make a better job of it; some are looking forward to a fashion parade, and some have just a kindly human interest, like the old lady who will say (and rightly!) when Jill appears, 'Don't she look luvly?'

Then your friends will want to be there. It is an important day in your life, and they will want to wish you well. They'll make all the old stock jokes and say the usual fatuous things, but they'll mean well.

Naturally, too, the parents will want to do you proud. You were in a bad temper when you wrote your letter, and more than half suggested that Jill's people were going to use the occasion as an opportunity to impress their neighbours, friends and relatives. Perhaps so. Which of us hasn't used occasions to impress other people? And they seem to have been uncommonly kind to Jill and you. After all, you know, it is partly their affair—this wedding. They did produce Jill for you—you've got to thank them for that. She's their daughter, and if they find any sort of satisfaction in launching her into matrimony with the flags out and the trumpets blowing, I shouldn't let that worry you. It will soon be over, anyhow! And you wouldn't take it as much of a compliment if they were so little pleased at handing their daughter over to you that they wanted to hush it up.

I think I detect just a suspicion of annoyance even with Jill because 'for no earthly reason that I can imagine, she seems to like it'. I shouldn't wonder. Even sensible girls do, you know, within limits. I shouldn't try to explain it. Just accept it. In some ways all these preparations, and the day itself, will mean more to Jill than to you. Don't be a boor and spoil everything for her. I thought I could detect in your letter a faint assumption of superiority, which won't do at all. There is a temptation at your age, if I may say so without sounding patronizing, to be uppish about conventions—which often have something in them. I remember I used to be quite contemptuous about strangers who raise their hats in the street when a funeral passes. But I've changed my ideas. Middle age mellows, you see. Well, enter into the whole business of the wedding with a good grace for the sake of others, if not for your own. Behave as though you're interested—and you probably soon will be.

I seem to have been blowing you up mildly, but all the same I was glad to sense the seriousness underlying your complaining. You are dead right in saying that a wedding ought not to be turned into a mere social function, and a lot are. Some couples get married in churches only because a church makes a better stage setting for the show than a register office. There's more scope for effects. That's disgusting. If you thought that was happening in your case, you'd be right to kick like mad. No couple have any business to get married in church unless the marriage service means *something* to them. I am not suggesting that everybody who is not a regular churchgoer should be married in a register office. Some people who have little enough to do with churches in the ordinary way do give religion an honest thought or two when marriage, birth and death enter into their lives. So if, even in a rather vague sort of way, they recognize the religious significance of their marriage, and want to ask God's blessing on it, by all means let them go to church for their wedding. If they don't, the register office is the proper place.

I hope the marriage service will mean a lot to you. Make yourself familiar with the words of it beforehand and think about what they mean. (I think, by the way, that there are things in some forms of the service which might very well be cut out. I expect Jill has already, quite properly, protested against promising to obey. If your marriage is the real thing, the word won't have any place in your vocabulary.) The parson, if he does his job efficiently, will go through the service with you beforehand, and you can ask him about anything you don't understand. You may think you will both be so nervous when the actual time comes that you will be in a sort of coma. I don't suggest you won't have any 'nerves', but you will be able to overcome them. When Jill finishes that interminable walk up the aisle, and stands by your side in that moment for which you have waited so long, concentrate on each other. Forget the crowd behind you. For the time being you are the only people who matter. Some people meet at the altar, and stare fixedly ahead with unseeing eyes as though they cannot recognize each other's existence until they have been introduced! And some others exchange a smile and a look of complete confidence and understanding. When that happens, one has the feeling that a real marriage service is about to begin. Think about the words of the hymn you are singing. (And do choose something reasonable.

Some people make the most awful howlers in the hymns they select, and in the music they ask the organist to play. You'd never believe the banal and sentimental stuff they hit on. There's no place for 'incidental music' in a service, and if music doesn't add to the real *value* of a service, it had better be cut out altogether.) Think, too, about the meaning of the words you say after the parson; don't just parrot them. They *mean* something. How much they mean (' . . . to have and to hold from this day forward, for better for worse, for richer for poorer, in sickness and in health, to love and to cherish, till death us do part, according to God's holy ordinance . . .') you can only discover as the years go on. Of course, they don't mean anything to people who are just entering into a convenient arrangement with each other, and intending to brush it on one side if they get tired of it. But it's a pretty big thing to make vows which are intended to last a lifetime, and it's right to make them in the presence of God and with a prayer for His help that they may be kept, not simply in letter but in *spirit*.

Well, I hope your wedding day will be one of the happiest and most significant days in your lives. But I think I know something of what Jill was feeling when she said she will be glad when it's all over. I expect the rush and excitement of it are a bit wearying. Actually some people find themselves a strange mixture of emotions on their wedding day. I don't imagine either Jill or you will be much troubled in that way, but it's a rather interesting point.

Some folk have told me they wanted to turn and run away from the church, though they really had no doubt that they were in love and that they were doing the right thing in marrying. It may be the feeling that they are doing something they won't be able to go back on which frightens them. It is just as if some little demon of doubt, knowing that people are in a more suggestible state when they are emotionally stirred, seizes the opportunity to whisper, 'Suppose it should turn out all wrong. Just suppose!' And then, of course, they want to panic. If that thought should pop up in your mind or Jill's, don't let it worry you. It has played the same trick before on plenty of people who have reached their golden weddings without ever regretting for a moment that they didn't turn and run! Of course, it would be a good thing if some people, who have just waltzed into marriage, did stop even at the church door and consider the possibility that they might be asking for trouble. But Jill and you have thought it all out. You know well enough that what you're going to do is right, and you're not really in two minds about it. So send the little demon packing!

With some people the worrying may have deeper roots. They are bothered by a sort of chronic uncertainty which always stirs up anxiety when they have to make a decision. That may be because they have a basic sense of insecurity going right back to childhood. It may have arisen because they did not feel certain of their parents' love, which is the foundation of the feeling of security a child must have if he or she is to face life with confidence. So they don't feel safe if they contemplate any change in their way of life.

Some other people, just *because* they are so much in love, and hope so much from their marriage, feel that something is bound to go wrong. They always do feel, if they are happy, that it can't last. Again the root of the trouble may be away back in childhood. They have developed a sort of apprehensiveness. They feel in their bones that things can't go right for them, though, as a matter of plain fact, they have not had any more bad luck than comes to most people. I have often found this apprehensiveness in grown men and women who had drunken fathers. As little children they would lie in bed listening for father to come home, and dreading the row or violence which might follow. Even when they were happy (at a party or something) the shadow was always there. Happiness, you see, wouldn't last. In some other cases, as children they had a deep sense of guilt, perhaps because of a resentment (very likely justified) against a parent. Feeling so dreadfully wicked, because every little child feels he *ought* to love, and not criticize, his parents, whatever they are like, they think they must be punished by some dreadful happening or by the loss of what they love and value.

If troubles like those are in people's minds, it isn't very surprising that they should make a point of bobbing up as the wedding day approaches. Unless there is some deep source of anxiety, there is no need to do anything about it; things will settle down all right. But if a man or girl faces marriage with anxiety for which there is no real cause, it is better to go to a psychologist and get things sorted out than to be dogged by it, because if it has the sort of roots I have been talking about, marriage in itself will not necessarily cure it.

Have you ever had the luck to see Thornton Wilder's play, *Our Town*? It contains an extraordinary scene in which Wilder tries to show what is going on in the minds of a young couple, very much in love, when they arrive at the church for their wedding. The girl, who is pretty het-up, says she never felt so lonely in her life. She clings to her father and wants to go home again with him—back to the old, familiar way of life. And, of course, she *is* lonely. Somebody says that even in the most intimate relationships people still remain 'dear strangers'. In the last analysis we have to face all the great experiences of life and death alone. (Religion has been defined as 'what a man does with his *solitariness*'—not his solitude. That's worth thinking about if you're interested. I'm sure it's a very profound remark.) The girl's father calls her lover and gives her over to him. And he seems to throw his love around her like a cloak and promises to look after her. Then her paralysing sense of loneliness goes. Happy and confident, they advance together to the altar to be joined in a union which will get as near to blotting out loneliness as is possible in this life.

P.S.—You aren't forgetting to attend to the legal details, are you? The law requires that the banns should be put up for three Sundays if you are being married in an Anglican Church; and if you are having the service in a Free Church, you have to give three weeks' notice to the local registrar. If you've slipped up on this, you'll have to get a licence, which will cost you more. And I hope you will give the parson as much notice as possible. Contrary to the ideas of some folk, a parson's diary gets pretty full up, and he can't always put off whatever engagement he has to suit their convenience. See that your best man settles up with the parson, the registrar, the verger, the caretaker, the organist and anybody else who is involved. It's part of his job.

XXVII

Where does religion come in?

MY suggestion that you should not overlook the religious significance of your marriage service has led you to ask that I will take
the matter a little further, and say something about the relation of
religion to the life which Jill and you will share in your new home.
I am glad to do so, because I believe it is tremendously important.
In fact, though we've talked about a lot of things, it's far and away
the most vital subject we've touched on in these letters. And I'm
glad it happens to have come in at the end, because we shall be
able to see how the things we've been discussing in previous
letters can all be taken up into religion—if it's a religion worth
having. You see, religion isn't a thing apart, as some people seem
to think. It is not just going to church on Sundays and then living
all the other six days as though you hadn't been. It is concerned
with every part of life, both personal and social. That's a colossal
subject, but I'm going to deal with it now only in so far as it
affects, or ought to affect, your home life.

Let me say, first, that religion is *an attitude to life*.

There are, broadly speaking, two possible attitudes. One is that
life means something; the other that it makes no sense at all.
Plenty of people in these days think there's no rhyme nor reason to
it. Seeing the mess and muddle we're in, that's not very surprising.
It all appears such a 'blooming, buzzing confusion' that it often
seems useless to look for plan or purpose in it anywhere. If any
power or force set the world going and brought us into being—
and I suppose somebody or something must have had a hand in it
since we certainly didn't do it ourselves—it surely must be blind
and stupid. Whatever it may be, there seems no reason to suppose
that it is aware of our loves and hates, our hopes and aspirations. If
it does know about them, it apparently doesn't care. Some people
think that man is just a queer sort of accident, a fluke, thrown up

by a blind process which hasn't the least idea what it is doing. Man is at the mercy of matter, and sooner or later he, and all he has striven for, will be flattened out as though a driverless steamroller had run amok. Well, that's pretty bleak, but wishful thinking won't get us anywhere, and, if that's the only possible view, we had better try to keep a stiff upper lip, square our shoulders and face up to it.

Now, if you keep your eyes fixed on one set of facts and refuse to look at any others, I think the view that life doesn't make sense will seem the only one possible. This world at the moment looks uncommonly like a madhouse, and, if you think long enough about all the evil, frustration and waste everywhere, and think *only* about that, you certainly won't find much reason for believing there's a God—at any rate, not one that you would care to know. I'm not denying that those things are facts. They *are*—and mighty hard ones, too. But I am saying that they are not the only facts. And it's just as one-eyed to leave these other facts out of account as it would be to pretend that the tough things were not there because you didn't like the look of them. Hatred and wickedness are facts all right, and we know, better than any generation since the world began, what they are and what they can do. But love and goodness are facts, too—the love Jill and you have for each other, and the love you will both have for your children when they come. You see, if there is hatred, there's also love; if there is cruelty, there's also kindness—amazing kindness and self-sacrifice sometimes; if there are lies, there's also truth; if there's ugliness, there is also beauty. Look at all the rotten and apparently senseless things in the world *by themselves*, and you'll throw out the idea of a good God, lock, stock and barrel. Then, if you turn your eyes to the good things, and the things which really seem to mean something (and you will if you're honest), you will have to bring back the idea of God to explain them. For, as somebody put it, if there's a problem of evil in the world, there's also a problem of good. If you can't explain the evil in the world, if there is a God, I don't know how you will set about explaining the good if there isn't.

Mind you, I'm not pretending that everything is as clear as daylight. It isn't to me, anyway, and, if anybody tells me it is to him, I shall suspect he's either a half-wit or the world's best wishful thinker. But I always remember the advice given by a philosopher. He used to say that, if a certain theory presents difficulties, it is worth while to have a good look at the alternative and see whether that presents greater difficulties. I admit, without any beating about the bush, that the belief that there is a God and that there's a purpose in life has difficulties—plenty of 'em! But I hold that to believe there is no God and no meaning lands you in worse ones. For man didn't bring himself into being, so, if there is no God who can be called a Person, man must have been produced by some force or turned out by a blind machine-like process. Now, I can't for the life of me see how a *personality* like man's, which can love and aspire and care for truth and beauty, can be produced by something which isn't personal, and which can't be conscious of love and truth and beauty. In particular, I can't understand how a blind, machine-like force managed to produce the finest of all personalities— Jesus Christ. I think the New Testament makes better sense that that. It says there is a God, who can be called a Father, and that God revealed what He is like in Christ, putting into Him everything which could be revealed within the limits of a human life. And the New Testament holds, further, that the value and purpose of life—of *every* life, including yours and Jill's—is revealed in Christ.

Well, you will have to come to some decision as to whether there is a God of this nature. You can, of course, refuse to make up your mind and to give a plain answer in so many words. But you will give your answer, nevertheless, by the way you live, for, as somebody says, a man can avoid making up his mind, but he can't avoid making up his life. Though I said that religion is an attitude to life, it is in the last analysis an attitude to God. The man who has a real religion is he who does not live for his own little selfish purposes, but who tries to discover and do the will of God in his home and in every other part of his life.

But I must switch off. You'll be saying I'm preaching! When I began I didn't mean to get launched into all this, but it wasn't much use to say I believe there is meaning and purpose in life unless I suggested some reason for it. Of course, I haven't been able to go into it properly. That will have to wait for a time when we can put pipes on and really get down to it. And I know you are fairly spluttering with questions you want to hurl at me. Why don't you go and fire them at a local parson? Try your own, of course, if you go to church often enough to call a particular parson 'yours'. But if the first man you go to doesn't ring the bell, have a bit of common sense about it and don't give up. A well-known journalist says that, when he was troubled by doubts in his young days, he took his difficulties to two clergymen. The first bade him sternly to put such sinful thoughts out of his mind. The other put his arm round his shoulders and said, 'My dear boy, don't worry. It will all come right in God's good time.' So, fed up with that, he decided to give religion a miss! Do you think if he had gone to two doctors, neither of whom could diagnose or cure his complaint, he would have decided there was nothing in medicine, and thenceforth have given it the go-by? Or, if something had gone wrong with his wireless set, and he had had the bad luck to run into two engineers who didn't know their stuff, would he have decided that there was nothing in radio anyhow and forthwith have smashed it up? There are parsons, plenty of them, who are intelligent and competent and who will treat your difficulties seriously.

Well, so much for that. For the rest of this letter I am going to assume that Jill and you believe that the Christian view is fundamentally sound. By 'the Christian view' I mean the faith that there is a God, Whose nature was revealed in the character, life, death, and resurrection of Jesus, and that He has a purpose which embraces every human life. Now, if you do believe that, you will adopt an attitude to life as a whole which follows from it.

First, an attitude to yourself. You won't imagine that you are here simply to grab for yourself and seek nothing but your own pleasure. Not many people would acknowledge that such blatant selfishness is their guiding principle, but their lives show it. And they go into marriage, as they go into everything else, asking what they can get out of it. Men of that kidney expect their homes to exist solely for their comfort and convenience. Their wives have no *raison d'être* except to slave for them, make themselves amusing, or serve as prostitutes (unpaid). It does not occur to them that their first question ought to be, not what they can get in marriage, but what they can give. Jesus said He came to serve, not to be served. That is a sound principle for home life. Only remember that service is, as Jesus meant it to be, the self-giving of love. Sometimes people serve others because it gives them a comfortable sense of superiority; they feel (perhaps unconsciously) that they have put the people they have helped into a position of inferiority or dependence. Real Christianity doesn't stand for that sort of thing—least of all in marriage. As between husband and wife there is neither superior nor inferior; they are two equal friends, who just give what they have to give because that is the way of love.

And in giving they find self-fulfilment. There has been an awful lot of talk about self-realization in recent years. That has often been a nice-sounding term for doing what you like and damn the consequences—to anybody else. In particular it has meant seeking sexual gratification wherever you fancy it or can get it. The truth is that nobody ever yet found self-realization that way. It is to be found not by a succession of sexual liaisons, which involve only the body and perhaps the most superficial part of the personality, but never the depths of it. Self-realization is found by entering into *real relationships* with others. The people who run from one sexual adventure to another often do it because they are afraid to commit themselves to any relationship which is more than casual and superficial. They are not really the bold, fearless people they would like you to suppose! Jesus uttered one of the fundamental laws inherent in the very nature of personality when He said that those who try to hang on to their lives (by which He meant much more than physical lives) will lose them, and that those who throw them away will find them. In other words, self-realization is not to be found by looking for it, by demanding that everybody should dance attendance on you and help you to inflate your own ego. You only come by it when, for the sake of love, you give yourself gladly to some person or cause without counting the cost. And the most complete self-fulfilment which human relationships can afford is to be found in a true marriage, because nowhere else is such complete self-giving possible.

Secondly, the Christian view of life means an attitude to other people. I suggested what that attitude is in an early letter, when I was talking about what true love means, but I didn't say then that it is derived from Christianity. I called it respect for personality, which means treating everybody as a person and not as a thing.

Yes, *everybody*—the butcher, the baker, and the candlestick-maker. There's no exception. There can't be, because they are all the children of God as you are yourself, and that gives every one of them an infinite value. He has given them all their own person-alities and their own lives to live, and we have no right to cramp the personality of even the least of them or imagine that he (or she) exists merely for our comfort or pleasure.

Now, other things besides charity begin at home, and respect for personality is one of them. Yet nowhere is it so easy to slip into the way of treating people as things or using them as tools. Think of that curse of so much family life—possessiveness. Even at this time of day there are husbands who treat their wives as mere chattels. They expect them to clean, and wash, and mend, and cook as services to be rendered to their overlords. They must always be on duty. They must, without fail, be home with the meal ready cooked, even if occasionally they would like to be out on their own pleasure. And they must be ready, at any time of the day or night, to submit to the sexual urges of the dominant male, whether they feel like it or not. They are not allowed any private or personal life, and they are not even granted that little bit of heavenly indepen-dence which would come from having an allowance, however small, which they could call their very own. Don't protest that there aren't such husbands, because there are. I've met them. But don't forget, Jill, that women can be every bit as possessive. Some of them won't let their husbands out of their sight, and demand that they shall dance attendance all the time until—if they are fools enough to give in to such petticoat government—they become the laughing-stock of all the men who know them.

What is even worse than all this is that the possessiveness of parents sometimes engulfs the children. Some men, who haven't the guts to chuck their weight about anywhere else, become tyrants at home and use their children as a means to gratify their sense of power. Sometimes children are overdriven in their school-work or in the making of a career to satisfy their parents' vanity. Sometimes, as I said in a previous letter, a mother (especially if she is unhappy in her love-life with her husband) does everything she can to bind her children to her with bonds that she hopes can never be broken. She will 'sacrifice' herself for them, spoil and coddle them, prevent them from doing things they ought to learn to do for themselves—in short, she will try every blessed thing she knows in order to make them dependent on her for life, while she protests that she is doing it all for love, and feels a martyr if they don't seem properly grateful to her for wrecking their lives! Worst of all, children are sometimes used as weapons in marital struggles, each parent trying to set them against the other. When your children come, for heaven's sake remember that they are not things, but personalities from the start, and that you must never *use* them in any sort of way. This is looking ahead a bit—but remember, especially when they are getting on towards manhood and woman-hood, that they have their own lives to live, and don't try unfairly to hold on to them. Somebody says that the first prayer of every parent ought to be, 'God give me the grace to let go'.

From the Christian angle, then, a home is not a place where a number of people are trying to see what each can get out of it by making use of the rest, but where parents and children all respect one another as personalities and where in friendship and loving ser-vice they achieve (as an inevitable by-product) self-realization. It is a *community* in which every member is encouraged to make his own contribution to the common life, and even the least gifted is made to feel that what he can give is valued and counts.

Thirdly, the Christian view of life means an attitude to the work and burdens of home. I have pointed out more than once that home life consists mainly of little things. A woman's life especially is made up of doing an endless succession of small jobs—washing, mending cooking, cleaning and so on *ad lib.*, or, as some would say, *ad nauseam*. Of course, some women ask nothing more of life than the daily round and common task, but to many that can be dread-fully monotonous and without significance. The whole outlook is altered if these everlasting chores can be linked up with a great principle which really does mean something. In St John's Gospel it is said that Jesus, knowing that 'He was come from God and went to God', rose from supper, took a towel, poured water into a basin and began to wash His disciples' feet. It is a flash of extra-ordinary insight which links up that service—the job of a menial slave—with His consciousness of His divine origin and destiny. Jesus saw nothing incongruous. Even the humblest details of life

were related to His love of men and God. We have to learn the
secret of taking up the chores and burdens of home into our love of
the family and of God. Then they have some meaning and value.
Of course, some women run their homes efficiently even though
they loathe and resent the whole business most of the time. They
have a pride in doing a job well however much they dislike it, or
they have a compelling 'sense of duty'. But there is all the difference in the world between the atmosphere of a home like that (it is
much more like a well-run hotel!) and one in which love is the
inspiration of everything. As somebody says, 'Duty makes us do
things well, but love makes us do them beautifully.'

Fourthly, the Christian view of life means an attitude to suffer-
ings and tragedies. Before the end of the story suffering and loss
will inevitably come your way. They are our human lot. Some
people crumple up under them; some become embittered. But
some face them with a wonderful courage and make something of
them. They grow into finer characters, acquire a deeper insight and
become more sympathetic and helpful to others.

You see, the Christian faith is that a power for living is available
to us if we will take it. Therefore we haven't got to live simply on
our own limited resources. Now, if we want to have that power one
thing we have to do is to learn how to pray. A lot of people have
the quite wrong notion that prayer means plaguing God to give us
something or do something for us. The most vital part of prayer is
actually the opening of our lives to God so that He can work in us
and through us. Jill and you will do well to build up a spiritual life
together. People are dreadfully shy about their religion, but it is a
good thing if husband and wife can talk to each other naturally
about their inmost thoughts. By sharing their faith and experience
they'll help each other a lot. Get into the way of reading and pray-
ing together. That doesn't mean you should never pray alone.
You'll need to be alone sometimes. If you feel you want some help
in learning how to pray, get hold of H. E. Fosdick's *The Meaning
of Prayer*. It gets down to the problems and difficulties in a way that
modern and intelligent people can appreciate. It's quite a small
book, but it's a gold-mine!

Well, a real religion is the best possible foundation for your
home life, but don't imagine it is concerned *only* with your family

circle. If it's the real thing, depend upon it your thoughts and aspirations and service will be pushed out beyond the four walls of your home. I read these words the other day, and they are so true that I pass them on to you to think over:—

You learn in the family to make the common life of love: you learn that it is not a thing that you can do alone. But when you have done this you are not at the end; you are at the beginning. Love is outward-turning, and as the love of man and woman is made by, as well as expressed in, the making of the family, so the love of the family is made by and expressed in the making of the world. If you love in God you will be saved from exclusiveness; and the closer you come to Him the wider your love will spread. If you can say implicitly of every action, 'I am doing this because I love the family and because in the family I love God', you will bring to the family an ever-increasing depth and intensity of life and power, and the power will more and more go out from you and enchant and help and console the world.

XXVIII

'Mixed' marriages

AT last you have asked me a question to which there is a short answer! You want to know whether it matters that Jill and you belong to different religious denominations. The answer to that is No! At any rate, it doesn't if you are sensible people. Mind you, I'm not saying that the things in which the Church of England, Methodists, Baptists, Congregationalists and the rest don't see eye to eye are of no consequence. Some silly people do say that, and seem to imagine that the various branches of the Christian Church are always getting across one another and squabbling about nothing. For the most part the denominations work together very well, but honest and intelligent people do think that their own particular denomination sees some bit of truth more clearly than the others, so they hold on to it, which you'll agree is right enough. So long as they're reasonable and tolerant, and realize that in the really big things Christians stand together, these differences don't matter much. No doubt it would be better if there were one great united Church, and that may come one day, but it won't be just yet. Jill and you can't wait for that. In the meantime you'll have to decide which Church you are going to belong to. It would be an awful pity if one of you went to one Church and the other to another. You would have divided your interests just where it is a grand thing to have them in common, and you would find the difficulties increased when the children arrived and you had to decide what you were going to do about them. And it wouldn't be a good solution to divide your loyalty between two Churches. You would not be likely to do justice to either of them.

It's just a case for talking the whole thing over together. It may be that one of you has by far the stronger denominational loyalty, which may well be allowed to settle the question, or perhaps there is a Church near your home which specially needs your help, or perhaps—oh! all sorts of things. You'll have to decide it for yourselves, but it shouldn't be difficult.

There's only one situation in which the question is of necessity a thorny one, and that is when one of the couple is a Roman Catholic. Then it's a different matter altogether. I have known a good many marriages in which Catholics have married Protestants which have turned out sheer tragedies. The Roman Catholic Church officially forbids 'mixed' marriages because, as an official publication puts it, they cause harm and suffering, because the Catholic may gradually lose his religion, because the children may be lost to the Church (i.e., the R.C. Church), and because they generally mean the cooling of the love of the man and the woman. Experience shows, it says, that mixed marriages are almost always unhappy. If, 'for serious reasons', the R.C. Church allows a mixed marriage, the Catholic must be free to practise the faith, the Catholic must try to convert the non-Catholic, the children must be brought up as Catholics, and the ceremony of the marriage must be Catholic. The non-Catholic will have to sign an agreement on the dotted line, and the Catholic will have to promise to do everything possible to convert the other partner. Pretty one-sided, isn't it? And humiliating enough for the poor Protestant if his religion happens to mean anything to him, for the differences of belief and religous conception between Catholic and Protestant are quite unlike those between the Protestant denominations. No doubt, when a couple are in love and see this bogy looming up and threatening to separate them, they try to persuade themselves that perhaps the difficulty won't be so tremendous after all, and that maybe the Roman Church doesn't mean all it says. But it does. And it's dead right, too, when it says that mixed marriages are almost always unhappy. A couple who are thinking of marrying on those terms ought to stop and think again, however much they are in love. At least they must go into it with their eyes open.

XXIX

'Bon voyage!'

THIS is the last letter I shall write to you before you're married, and it brings you my good wishes for every kind of happiness. You have taken your marriage seriously—but, thank goodness, not too seriously! You have done all you could to prepare yourselves for what somebody has called 'the most exacting career imaginable'. You deserve to be happy, and you will be.

But a wise man once said that ninety-nine marriages out of every hundred have their difficult patches, and you would be rash to assume that yours will be the hundredth. You'll take most of your difficulties in your stride. Just in case you should strike a really sticky patch somehow, can I give you one last word of advice—if you can stand it?

You see, a couple sometimes get to the point where they can't sort out their difficulties without somebody to help them. Even with the best will in the world they talk and talk and go round in circles. Presently they become so exasperated and discouraged that there isn't much goodwill left, and they start on mutual recriminations which grow like snowballs. They can't see their problems straight, and they never will unless somebody, who comes into the situation from outside, can help them to do it. So don't let a bother, whether it's sexual maladjustment or anything else, get chronic before you do something about it. Doctors are always saying that if only people would come to them in time they could cure a lot of cases (of cancer, for example) which have to be given up as hopeless. And those of us who try to help people with marriage difficulties often think—it's not much use to say it!—'If only you had come five, ten or twenty years ago you could have been helped to get straightened out and have saved yourselves a lifetime of unhappiness.' Sometimes a couple will seek help *together*—they're the really wise ones. Sometimes one of the partners won't co-operate, and the other won't open out to anybody because it seems like disloyalty. It *is* disloyalty if you go around talking of your marriage troubles to everybody. But it isn't anything of the kind if you go to somebody and give a plain, unvarnished tale, trying to tell the whole truth so that you can be helped, and not simply trying to make your own case good or to get sympathy as a poor, ill-used creature. Often, when the trouble is sexual, a couple won't breathe a word to anybody because they think they will look incompetent or silly. Many a man, who could easily have been cured, has remained sexually impotent for years at the cost of his wife's suffering and his own humiliation, because of the quite false notion that a doctor or other adviser would think him a poor specimen and only half a man.

Well, then, don't put off getting help if you need it. But go to the right person. It must be somebody competent, and it must be somebody who will keep your confidence. It may be a doctor, a parson, or an experienced friend—though do make sure your friend is competent. All the kind feelings in the world won't help if knowledge is what's needed. Or go to the local Marriage Guidance Council if there is one where you happen to be living. Very soon there will be one established in all the bigger towns, with a qualified counsellor, who will treat all you say as strictly confidential, and who will be able to put you in touch with a specialist consultant if you need one. Already in this way thousands of marriages have been mended, and thousands more have been saved from ever breaking up. I've only written all this just in case. I don't expect Jill and you are ever likely to want help. If every couple prepared themselves for marriage as well as you two have, there wouldn't be much for Marriage Guidance Councils to do in the way of salvage!

Well, go ahead with absolute confidence in each other. You're setting out on an unknown journey, but you'll make grand travelling companions, and I hope the journey will be a long one. You'll find a wonderful happiness in sharing the joys of the road, and if now and again life knocks you about a bit you'll have each other.

Good luck—and God bless you!